Ethics across the Curriculum

Ethics across the Curriculum

A Practice-Based Approach

Michael Boylan and James A. Donahue

LEXINGTON BOOKS
Lanham • Boulder • New York • Oxford

LEXINGTON BOOKS

Published in the United States of America
by Lexington Books
An imprint of The Rowman & Littlefield Publishing Group, Inc.
4501 Forbes Boulevard, Suite 200, Lanham, Maryland 20706

PO Box 317
Oxford
OX2 9RU, UK

British Library Cataloguing in Publication Information Available

Library of Congress Cataloging-in-Publication Data

Boylan, Michael, 1952–
    Ethics across the curriculum : a practice-based approach / Michael Boylan and
James A. Donahue
        p. cm.
    Includes bibliographical references and index.
    ISBN 0-7391-0573-6 (alk. paper)—ISBN 0-7391-0769-0 (pbk. : alk. paper)
    1. Ethics. I. Donahue, James (James A.) II. Title.

BJ1012 .B617 2003
170'.71'1—dc21   2002151168

Printed in the United States of America

♻™ The paper used in this publication meets the minimum requirements of American
National Standard for Information Sciences—Permanence of Paper for Printed Library
Materials, ANSI/NISO Z39.48–1992.

Contents

Preface

This book is a collaboration between a philosopher with theological interests (Boylan) and a theologian with philosophical interests (Donahue). We began this particular project when we planned and presented a summer faculty ethics seminar at Marymount University in 1996. In various iterations of the project our plan and mission became increasingly clear: to introduce faculty in other disciplines and in professional schools to concepts in ethics so that they might integrate to some degree value elements present in but not often discussed in their disciplines.

We presented the seminar six times. Many of the thoughts in this volume in one way or another reflect the effects of this interaction. The voice in this book is thus two voices that are very similar at times, but never exactly identical. The differences are due to our fundamental approaches (philosopher vs. theologian) and to the manner in which we apply our individual strengths to the project at hand. In order to maintain the integrity of each of our visions, we have made no attempt to correct minor discrepancies between our two methodologies. The reader should note that Donahue was the lead author in chapters 1, 3, and 6, while Boylan was the lead author in chapters 2, 4, and 5. The last two chapters are without lead authors.

However, our similarities are much more apparent than our differences. Both of us seek a way to integrate ethics and discussions of value into the entire university curriculum. To this end we have organized the book in the following fashion.

In chapters 1 and 2 we examine the university as it stands and how it might be different if our proposal for ethics across the curriculum were to be adopted. We raise various issues in the context of objections and replies. One of the most challenging objections is that we are taking time away from content-based instruction and transferring it over to some more subjective, irrelevant material. Our position is that value examination is not a "watering down" of the teaching of these subjects but rather an "enrichment" that prepares students to be better, more integrated people in their future careers.

Chapters 1 and 2 are meant to break the ice and introduce the reader to what we are proposing and why it is a fulfillment and not diminution of *human actor — values + understandings about facts that make up the world.*

the university's mission.

In chapters 3 and 4 the concepts of narrative and the worldview approach are presented. Both are holistic devices that aspire to characterize the human agent as being more than a mere "thinking machine." Instead, the human agent is depicted as being a composite of various values and understandings about facts that characterize the world. It is in these chapters that the fundamental theoretical approach that underlies the book is enunciated.

This approach is given greater specification in chapters 5 and 6 as the realm of professional ethics and the embedded theory of value are introduced. These aspire to act as linking principles that can move us from theory to practice. The move from theory to practice is traditionally one of the most vexing problems in ethics.

Our presentation concludes with two chapters that address specific problems. In chapter 7 the question of religious values is addressed. This is a very troublesome question in modern America (and in other areas of the world). Clearly, most people profess to believe in a monotheistic religion. Yet, at the same time, the values that those religions profess are generally given little attention by those studying ethics. This is because there is so much disagreement about religion that most ethicists wish to simplify the process and consider only secular discussions of the "right and wrong of human action." This chapter provides a vision that accommodates both the humanists and the theists in the context of both public and private colleges and universities.

In chapter 8 a provisional vision is set out of just what might be involved in setting out a plan for ethics across the curriculum in any university. Through using the structure of stakeholder analysis, various viewpoints are explored.

This book will be of interest to:

(a) Those who are interested in how we might be able to introduce discussions of ethics, religion, and other values to college and university students.

(b) Those who want to explore how ethics, religion, and other values permeate areas of thought that have often been considered to be value-free.

(c) Those who have always been interested in ethics, but have despaired because of its lack of connection between theory and practice.

shared community worldview imperative → Polit. → social organization

worldview approach → Personal worldview imperative → lead an examined life

This book is unique in the way it:

(a) Introduces an integrative approach to studying ethics (and other values). This is the worldview approach. In the individual realm this translates to the creation of a Personal Worldview Imperative that exhorts people to lead examined lives. In the social/political realm this translates to the creation of the Shared Community Worldview Imperative. This dictum lays the groundwork for a comprehensive theory of social and political organization.

Look at how values ∧ facts coexist in complex relation

(b) Uses narrative to examine and illumine the fundamental and primary issues involved in ethical inquiry. This device illumines how values and fact coexist in a very complex relation.

(c) Creates a mechanism (the embedded-values approach) that allows the practitioner seamlessly to move from theory to practice.

Embedded values approach

(d) Develops a theory of ethos and professionalism that is normative rather than merely descriptive in nature.

In the end this book seeks to stimulate reflection about the role of values in education and how we might do more. In today's world we are increasingly becoming a population of specialists who are so narrow in our focus that we lose the balance of character that has been much advocated throughout history. One remedy for this problem is for colleges and universities to take seriously the challenge of developing the whole person. It is our contention that by paying attention to educating the whole person that we will develop future citizens who are better able to balance the practical, professional, and moral demands of our modern age.

As in any project such as this there are many individuals to thank. The authors want to thank in particular the faculty of Marymount University who have participated in the summer seminars on ethics across the curriculum. We also are grateful to our reviewers, especially Gabriel Palmer-Fernandez and Lisa Newton. We are appreciative as well of the superb editorial and technical support given by Laura Peck and Kathryn Bellm of the Graduate Theological Union. They have helped the manuscript become a reality. Jim would like to acknowledge the patience, support, and encouragement of his spouse Jane, which have been invaluable to the work of this project. He thanks his sons Nick and Luke for their patience as well. Michael also is grateful to his family (Rebecca, Arianne, Seán, and Éamon) who nurture, support, and put up with his many eccentricities.

Develop the whole person → future citizens

Chapter 1
Ethics in the University Context

Ethics has become somewhat of a cottage industry recently in the United States. It is hard to go into a bookstore these days without finding numerous offerings about the ethical challenges of the times on prominent display.[1] It is even harder to watch television without seeing stories abounding about ethical struggles and conflicts of either a personal or social nature. Stories of international conflict, religiously inspired violence, personal moral character, economic prosperity and political culture wars, or corporate responsibility are at the forefront of our public conversations. The Sunday *New York Times Magazine* even has a weekly column entitled "Ask the Ethicist" in which an ethics expert answers queries from readers about everyday ethical conflicts they encounter. It is no wonder that the question of ethics has penetrated to the heart of the university and we find ourselves in a time in which faculty, students, administrators, and the general public are asking about the role of the university in educating about matters of ethics.

This book examines the role of ethics in the university. Should it be taught? Can it be taught? How should it be taught? Who should teach it? What are the goals of teaching ethics? What should its content be? These are very complex questions and yet they need to be asked and answered by every institution of higher education today. The intention of this book is to indicate how a university can determine the appropriate place of ethics education in the overall context of university life, in particular in the curriculum. It answers the basic questions about whether ethics should be taught affirmatively, but asserts that there is no one absolutely right way of doing this. Rather, this book outlines the critical issues at stake in the matter of ethics education across the curriculum and examines how ethics might be taught in ways that not only preserve the integrity of the existing academic disciplines in the curriculum but enhance the quality and effectiveness of the curriculum overall. This book is the collaboration of two professors, one a philosopher and the other a theologian, who show how their own disciplines can collaborate in furthering ethics education. It is intended for anyone who has a practical interest in these matters—professors, students, and college administrators. The book is meant to be both practical and theoretical. It provides recom-

mendations about how decision makers can implement practical strategies for adopting ethics education in the curriculum.

Ethics and the Purposes of the University

A discussion of the role of ethics in the university must begin with an
understanding of the fundamental goals and purposes of the university
and about the aims and goals of higher education in general. There is not
one right answer or correct viewpoint on this matter. Colleges and universities differ by type and have differing missions and goals, and within
each of these there are different units, schools, and departments that have
distinct purposes. These units will think about ethics education in somewhat particular ways depending on their own outlooks. Professional
schools of law, business, and medicine will view the ethical components
of their curricular offerings differently than will general liberal arts undergraduate institutions. Let us begin, then, with as broad and fundamental a notion of higher education as possible.

The etymology of the word "education" provides an appropriate starting point. The Latin root of education is *educare,* meaning "to lead out."
This leading out can be seen as a movement from ignorance to knowledge as it was to Plato,[2] from old traditions and ways of knowing to new
ways of construing reality, from one skill set to another, from one set of
competencies to a new one. All of these understandings suggest a movement in which the student is led from one level of understanding to one
in which there is an enhanced and improved quality of knowledge and
insight. It also implies that this movement is not passive but active. The
educator is one who takes leadership in the leading-out process. It is the
teacher or mentor who introduces the student to knowledge and information or puts in place a process that will provide a more developed and
perfected way of knowing for the student. But this movement from ignorance to knowledge does not entail merely the possession of facts by the
students, or the transmission of information from teacher to student, but
also implies the ability of students to appropriate this knowledge in a
way that will enable them to apply it to new sets of facts and experiences
that expand the mind and knowledge of the learner. There is something
most crucial that goes on in the process of leading out and being led out.
It has to do with what happens to the person in the educational process. It
entails a level of participation on the student's part in the process of
learning.

Aristotle distinguishes between three modes of knowledge: *theoria, praxis*, and *technē*.[3] *Technē* is the type of knowledge in which the knower takes information or an idea and forms it in accord with a preconceived plan, for example in building a structure or designing an edifice of some type. *Praxis* refers to a knowledge in which the knower participates in the activity of the knowing to the extent that there is a kind of lived learning and personal transformation that occurs in the process of participating and identifying with the object of knowledge that is being studied. It is a practical knowing that involves the person in a relationship with the known object. The participant-observer methods of anthropologists and some sociologists are an example of this. *Theoria* builds on the previous kinds of knowing in that the knower interacts with the object of knowledge to the point that the knower comes to realize and grasp the ends and ultimate forms of the object in a completely new way. In *theoria* the knower undergoes a change and comes to stand in a different perspective to the ideas at hand in the process of the learning. True knowledge is the process in which one comes to grasp the truth and insight of ideas by engaging with them and allowing oneself to be moved by them to the point where one comes to a new form of understanding.

Educators in higher education make many claims as to what the goals of college and university learning are. There are some who claim that college education is meant to prepare students for the marketplace and to that end the best use of the classroom is to transmit to students the information and skills that they will need in a competitive world.[4] Others claim that the aim of university education is to receive the best ideas from the historical traditions of many disciplines with the goals of amassing an information base that can be applied to new situations in the present and the future. Still others view the university as a place where ideas are valued as ends in themselves, independent of their uses.

Ethics education across the curriculum presumes that there is a dynamic relationship between the knower and the known and that it is essential to education that there be an active form of participation of the knower in the process of learning. Ethics education focuses on ideas and theories of the right and the good but it never does this in a completely theoretical and abstracted way. It presumes a situation of dialogue in which the student is challenged to engage the ideas at hand and to come to some critical appropriation of them for the purposes of applying these insights to the issues and situations of the present and future.[5]

Ethics education presumes that the role of the university is to engage and challenge students to stand in a new place with regard to the ideas *develop whole the student* (handwritten)

that objects of knowing that they encounter. Universities are not merely transmitters of facts and information from the past. They are dynamic centers of inquiry where students and faculty come together to examine ideas and issues in ways that will be transformative of the individuals who engage in the inquiry. The educator Paulo Freire distinguished "banking education," in which faculty "deposited" information in the students who acted as passive receivers of ideas and information, from "education for transformative practice," in which students engaged the ideas and the context in which they were developed and in the process of learning became transformed to engage as active participants, creators, and learners in the world of which they are a part.[6] Universities are dynamic institutions in the world in which we live. The learning that takes place there must reflect the shifting and changing context of our world.

The Harvard educator Henry Rosovsky states in his oft-cited book *The University: An Owner's Manual* that education is not a science and that any static definition of the goals of education is impossible.[7] He offers a definition by José Ortega y Gasset as a powerful understanding of the aims of general education. "General education means the whole development of an individual, apart from his occupational training. It includes the civilizing of his life purposes, the refining of his emotional reactions, and the maturing of his understandings about the nature of things according to the best knowledge of our time."[8]

While there are other forms of education besides general education, the idea of education as leading out from ignorance to true wisdom requires an understanding of the student's being transformed through active engagement as a whole person with the ideas and concepts that are presented and discovered in the relationship between teacher and students. In ethics education to be led out means to engage actively the theories, ideas, and concepts of the good that are presented in the learning process and to appropriate them critically in application to the situations of the day. In this process a transformation occurs in the student's mode of moral knowing.

If education is about the way that the student as a "whole person" in his or her life's context develops a set of critical skills and insights for his or her life's work, ethics across the curriculum as a discipline and a field of inquiry must engage the full range of the student's ways of knowing the good, the valuable, and the worthwhile. It must be not only an intellectual undertaking but it must also engage the imaginative, psychological, aesthetic, and spiritual aspects of a student's experience.

Understanding Ethics: Ethics as Process / Ethics as Content

[handwritten margin note: Ethics = the process of reflection on the moral meaning of actions.]

We define ethics as the process of reflection on the moral meaning of actions.[9] This definition is meant to be broad and foundational and to incorporate several components of ethics education. Ethics is first and foremost a process. It is not simply a study in which one grasps some fundamental truths in one static moment of time and applies these in a deductive manner in other aspects of one's life. It is, rather, an ongoing process in which one is constantly engaged in a dialogue with ideas, people, history, traditions, other disciplines, and other students. Ethics is not a discrete body of knowledge that one simply acquires for application and use in particular situations. It entails the ongoing appropriation of ideas of the good as they relate to the changing situations, contexts, and developments in individuals' and groups' lives.

Ethics reflects on actions—the actions of individuals and groups. Its goal is to assess these actions in light of their "moral" meaning. Actions can have several kinds of meanings. They can have a sociological or psychological meaning, biological or physical significance, among others, depending on the lens of analysis that is used in the investigation. Ethics as a discipline uses the lens of "moral" analysis, that is, the way that actions are understood from the perspective of a concept of "the good."[10] The idea here is that actions are better or worse morally depending on how they fit with a notion of what we—as individuals, as societies, as humans, as believers or nonbelievers—understand to be what constitutes a state or condition of ultimate value and worth. In other words, the idea of the good is not necessarily a fixed notion, but rather one that is constantly being developed, constructed, received, and shaped about what we believe captures the best of human thought about what is of ultimate significance and meaning. There are multiple understandings of what constitutes the good and ethics examines ideas of the good and the right and makes determinations as to which notions are most adequate, which notions are the most perduring, and which ones are those that have authoritative currency in the world in which we live. This exploration is never one that is complete or finished. It is a process.

There are other ways that the task of ethics can be formulated that are consistent with the understanding of ethics that has been outlined here. Ethics entails the evaluation of actions in light of what is authentically human or in light of what is most constructive for human action, or what is most consistent with religious or philosophical beliefs that individuals or groups believe capture the fundamental truths of human existence. Ethics assesses the ways that actions are assessed in light of some fundamental or comprehensive notion of what constitutes the good.

What are the implications of these ideas for ethics across the curriculum in the university? They suggest first that ethics must be cross-disciplinary. While the disciplines of philosophy and theology are the home disciplines for ethics, the very nature of the enterprise suggests that these disciplines must be in collaboration and dialogue with other disciplines throughout the university. Since the idea of what is good is a comprehensive and integrative notion, only by using multiple lenses of analysis is it possible to develop a view of morality that is sufficiently inclusive to grasp the realities that it seeks to capture. Ethics, or reflection on the good, is something that penetrates to the heart of every discipline and every type of education. There is always some operant notion of the good at work in the process of any academic inquiry. Ethics across the curriculum examines the many ways that this notion operates in the university curriculum so that students and teachers can develop views that represent and capture the fullest and most adequate notion of what is of value that is possible to be grasped.[11]

Some examples will help to clarify the ways that ethics issues are intrinsic constantly in university education and why ethics across the curriculum is both an important and necessary undertaking. When students read fiction in their English classes each novel that they read will depict characters, situations, stories, and events that will have some moral quality to them. They will capture an idea of what is good or bad, what is a preferred action or character, or will at least examine some possible interpretations of what is good or bad. The point of the analysis will not necessarily be to discern the good and bad, but rather to recognize that in every story discussed some idea of the good is at work, some vision of possible states of affairs is presented which captures an idea of the good. The point of ethics education is not to capture in a reductionistic manner a view of "the" good but rather to give students the critical skills to see that notions of the good and of value are ever present in literature and to expose them to the issues at stake in their reading and interpretations.

Courses in the natural sciences are filled with ethical content. In the biological, chemical, technological, or physical sciences, there are assumptions about possible desirable or achievable states of the natural order. Students examine in their course work principles and theories that propose views of the way things are or the way things could be in the natural order. Intrinsic to these inquiries are assumptions and questions about how particular ideas, theories, and worldviews are to be valued. For students it is essential that they have the tools and the skills to be able to make judgments about these value questions. Scientific inquiry also frequently involves experiments and actions that will have powerful and far-reaching consequences. The impacts of scientific decisions for the environment, for biological and physical health, for societies and cultures, and for the way humans live are enormous. The potential consequences of scientific decisions raise an array of issues that students in science courses need to examine and understand.

Professional education in law, medicine, business, and engineering, as well as other professions, also contains issues of great ethical importance. Each profession contains ideas and views of the world based on a set of assumptions that are the foundation of that profession. The legal profession makes assumptions about the role of law in a society;[12] engineers make assumptions about how structure, form, and design are to be used for human use; business makes assumptions about how economics and commerce serve to provide the foundational dynamics for human interaction and exchange. Professions have ethical content in two ways: in the views they present according to the assumptions they work with, and the consequences that ensue in light of the decisions that members of a profession actually make. Students who are being trained in the professions must have an idea of what these issues are and be able to assess what is at stake in these issues from an ethical point of view. Professional decisions will convey an idea of the good that is critical for both the practitioner and the social world of which they are a part.

What Ethics Education Is / What It Is Not: Some Critical Distinctions

There is confusion around ethics education in that erroneous assumptions are often made about its goals and methods. There is a tendency to conflate ethics education with other endeavors. Some critical distinctions will help sharpen the understanding.[13]

1. Theoretical versus Practical Ethics

Academics frequently make distinctions between the theoretical and the applied aspects of intellectual educational discourse and there is considerable disagreement as to which is the most appropriate or desirable form. Theoretical approaches favor attention to the history of ideas and the conceptual issues that frame a particular discipline. Courses with this bias would prioritize the use of texts and focus more on matters of interpretation, methodology, and intellectual coherence as the essence of a course's substance. Applied approaches are those that traditionally focus on the practical application of ideas to concrete situations in a particular arena of human activity. The use of case studies and concrete examples drawn from contemporary experience will be the focal point of most of these courses.

Proponents of ethics education reflect the same split in their preferences for the appropriate approach to teaching ethics. Is the point of teaching ethics to grapple with the history of ideas about ethics and to be clear about the conceptual foundation of ethical activity or is the point more to find ways of resolving real-life situations? Is the reason for teaching ethics to develop knowledge about what constitutes the good and the right or is it to realize how ideas about the good and the right can be used to address specific problems in the lives of individuals and societies? Some ethics courses focus on the solutions to vexing moral problems of the day; others search for a conceptual clarity in ethical thinking in approaching problems.

The view of this book is that both of these approaches are essential to effective ethics education and that to dichotomize these is not a useful way of understanding ethics education. Ethical theory is valuable in that it provides help in making real moral choices. Real moral choices provide the context in which we think about theory and how to conceptualize a moral framework. Theory and practice are two interdependent ways of construing the task of ethical discourse and ethics education. Theory helps to clarify the concrete and the particular; real cases provide ways of helping to think more coherently about the concepts that frame our understanding of the moral life. A solid course in ethics must attend to both aspects of this moral dynamic. It must address theory as well as application.

2. Professional Education versus General Education

The distinction here is between students in professional or pre-professional school contexts and those in a liberal arts, humanities-based curriculum. The concern of ethics in professional schools is to provide an understanding of the moral challenges and conflicts that arise in the conduct of professional activity, and its aim is to give students the tools for making good moral choices in their future professional careers and to inform them on the state of the art in understanding certain kinds of moral conflicts. Courses frequently focus on examples and case studies from within a profession and the goals are quite practical and concrete. The conceptual foundations for these courses frequently will be the existing standards, principles, or statutes that have been articulated by a profession as providing the parameters and context for making moral choices.

General education approaches are more concerned with the larger ethical and philosophical contexts in which professional activity takes place.[14] Its focus is typically on a level of analysis that challenges some of the existing ethical frameworks of the professions and it situates the professional in a larger worldview, one that is derived from the larger social context and is shaped by fundamental insights about the nature and purpose of human action more generally. These courses will draw frequently on philosophical, theological, or sociological frameworks. Such courses tend to be more critical of professional choices and will challenge the professionals' understanding of the problems they are facing. Contextualizing professional choices in law in a comprehensive framework of social justice, for example, would typify a more general educational approach. The course might spend the predominance of time attending to the adequacy of ideas as to what constitutes social justice. The application of the concept would derive from this more fundamental goals and purposes.

The focus of this book is on an integration of the two polarities. Professionals are best served by attending to the larger constructs and understandings that frame their moral choices. Theory is best served by understanding the exact nature of the dynamics and tensions that constitute the professions themselves, which arise in practical cases. The call in this book is for methodologies and course approaches that can be inclusive of the need for professionals to know the specifics of their conflicts and choices but to understand a larger moral frame of reference as well. We will outline how to achieve this integration in the course of our analysis.

Combine sen. ed. ∧ prof. ed.

3. Normative Ethics versus Metaethics

Some educators argue that the proper focus of an ethics course is on questions about ethics and others believe that it is on providing normative guidance about what ought to be done in particular contexts and what principles ought to govern human action.[15] Metaethics is concerned with questions about the limits and possibilities of ethics and philosophical questions about whether ethics is even possible and desirable. There are those who contend that modern ethics has taken a far too dramatic practical turn and that the contemporary preoccupation with solving problems negates a more fundamental and necessary inquiry. Proponents of normative ethics take the position that an exclusive concentration on abstract questions ignores the more obvious need in our time to find ideas in ethics that will give us the ability to make important and necessary decisions to live humanely and justly in light of our deepest possibilities and aspirations.

The bias of this book is towards *normative* ethics. Ethics across the curriculum addresses a set of practical issues and needs in the disciplines and professions. It searches for answers to the question "What ought I/we to do or to be?" And yet while our concern is practical it understands that morally adequate answers to practical problems can be achieved only when the practical derives from well-grounded first principles and fundamental concepts of the good. Effective ethics education must resist the temptations of reductionism and dichotomous thinking. Our approach is integrative and committed to the potential for bringing conflicting approaches to ethics together within a workable framework and methodology.

4. Philosophical versus Religious Ethics

Philosophers and theologians will argue about whether the proper grounding for ethics is most appropriately philosophical or religious. Is religious belief and faith necessary as the basis for moral action or can one base an ethics on the foundations of philosophical reason without reference to some concept of the divine? Are these two disciplines mutually exclusive as the foundations for ethics? Again, the historical debate has dichotomized the two disciplines. This issue is particularly relevant with regard to the setting in which the ethics education takes place. In a public university setting, for example, there will be constraints on the way that religious beliefs in a normative sense are viewed and incorporated into the inquiry about ethics. In private or religiously affiliated institutions there tend to be fewer constraints on how one addresses questions of religious belief.[16]

This book is the product of a philosopher and a theologian. It is based on the belief that while these two disciplines are distinct and have their own canons of authority and authenticity there is common ground on which the foundations of ethics are built. We assert that all claims about ethics must be justified on terms that are rationally defensible and logically coherent. We assert as well that religious claims about ethics derive in part from philosophical warrants. The classical understanding of theology as "faith seeking understanding" requires a comprehensive and integrative understanding of how faith and reason are at work simultaneously in the comprehension of moral insight. We believe that ethics education must incorporate understandings of both these two disciplines and develop a way that the two can be seen as complementary and collaborative rather than as conflictual and contentious.

5. Ethics versus Values Clarification / Normative versus Descriptive Ethics

Ethics education searches for insights about what I/we ought to do and provides the basis upon which moral choices can be developed and justified. It is dramatically different from an analysis in which the decisions and choices that individuals and groups make are presented and described without an attempt to provide the grounding reasons for these actions. Descriptive ethics or "values clarification" is the analysis in which there is little or no attempt to critically assess and justify action and values.[17] These approaches simply assert or posit a value and/or a decision and indicate that the value is self-evidently true or authentic and that following this value is non-problematic. Values clarification typically does not deal with conflicts in values, the prioritization of values, or the justification of moral claims. It describes what people believe and actually do in a moral sense.

Ethics is the inquiry that critically assesses the claims that individuals and groups make for their actions. It analyzes the moral justifications and provides criteria for assessing the adequacy of the moral claims made. It examines notions of the good with a view to determining which actions are most consistent with these ideas. In doing this it provides the basis for discriminating among rival moral claims. Ethics education in the university is premised on the idea that the goal of education is to give students skills to make critical choices about those actions that are most constructive for human living. Simply describing how one views the world and what values one believes in does not help to achieve that goal. Rather, values clarification, while a helpful exercise in enabling students to articulate their views and come to know where they stand on value-laden issues, does not provide the substantive critical, ethical approach that is a fundamental requirement of a university curriculum.

6. Ethics versus Character Formation

There is a strong movement in our society today to address issues of character formation in our schools.[18] Cultural critics contend that we have lost our moral fiber as a society and that we need to reintroduce notions of right and wrong to our children to ensure that they will learn how to do the right thing. The impetus for many of these contentions is the belief that the adults of today, the present generation of public and private leaders, as well as the presentation of values in the media, have not set examples that are worthy of emulation by today's children. It is also born of a strong ideological desire to pass on one set of philosophical, political, economic, and social points of view to the next generation.

The idea of character formation as a way of doing ethics is based on the erroneous assumption that people can be shaped and formed in ways that are consistent with the ideas and views of the ones who are doing the shaping. There is seldom in this approach a full appreciation for the critical assessment of values and the internalization and appropriation of these values by the ones who are being taught. It sometimes comes from a desire on the shaper's part to control and dominate the one being shaped. The complexity of cultural values and the process of how these values are communicated from one individual or group to another is an intricate and involved phenomenon.

The goal of university education is not to form character, although surely in the educational process character is formed, values are transmitted, and individuals appropriate a set of beliefs and convictions. A university curriculum is not however the place where the character formation process occurs directly. The role of an academic discipline is to analyze critically the values and assumptions of a society and a culture. The student, in the process of being led out, is the one whose educational task is to assess and appropriate a set of values that are coherent and defensible. Ethics education does this, but this is not character formation.

7. Ethics versus Catechesis/Inculcation

There are similarities between catechesis and character formation as assumed understandings of ethics education. Catechesis, more properly a term that has reference to religious education, is the form of education in which students are introduced to the traditions, doctrines, narratives, historical-truth claims, and people of a religious tradition and learn from the elders the ways of the community or the tradition.[19] There is a legitimate role for this type of education, but it is not properly the role of the university to engage in such activity, except in religious colleges with a self-conscious institutional mission and commitment to catechesis. The university's role is to introduce the student to the intellectual traditions of a culture or cultures, and give the student the appropriate tools to be able to make sense of and critically appropriate a moral worldview. Even in universities where there is religious affiliation the more specifically religious or catechetical functions of transmission of traditions must be differentiated from the educational and intellectual tasks of the academic community.

Ethics across the Curriculum: Three Arenas
of Moral Discourse

Professors are confronted with ethical issues in several places in the university context—in the classroom, in the disciplines, and in the professions and applied settings. A thorough approach to ethics across the curriculum should be able to address the full range of ethical challenges.

In the Classroom
College students come to every course and every class with some kind of moral worldview or a set of guiding principles and beliefs upon which they base and justify their actions. Sometimes this moral sense is explicit and a set of moral principles is in place, of which the student is fully cognizant. Sometimes the moral sense is not fully articulated and is inchoate in its form. The developmental process is key to understanding the nature of ethics in the curriculum. Professors often get deluged with

ethical questions about the material being studied. They are frequently not prepared to wade into what they perceive as the treacherous waters of ethical discourse. If a university is to be true to its mission to develop in students the skills necessary to construct a more humane world for the future, it must necessarily allow and encourage students to explore ethical issues. This book seeks to provide professors the skills they need to address ethical issues as they arise in the classroom. We will provide a framework and foundational insights and knowledge that will be useful to them in this regard. This will entail giving basic knowledge about how to apply a moral or ethical lens to the material that is used in the classroom. It will require an understanding of the foundational insights in the history of modern (and classical) ethical theories as well.

In the Disciplines

Every academic discipline has internalized understandings of the good. There are a set of value assumptions that operate in any field of inquiry and these are typically based on ideas about the way things work, the values that operate among people in human interaction, or the way that knowledge is derived. There is a moral worldview implicit in the way that disciplines are organized and constructed. There is an implicit logic as well that frames how inquiry is to proceed in a discipline and spells out criteria that will be used for discriminating among particular claims of interpretation and adequacy. These assumptions and this logic are communicated in the teaching process and can have a powerful influence in the construction of the moral worldview of the student.

Some examples of this discipline-specific valuation include the way that the natural sciences use the scientific method that provides an empirical and data-driven basis for the justification and support of truth claims and assertions of fact and value. In the natural sciences the verifiability of all claims depends on their ability to be supported by empirical data. While this is not problematic from an academic perspective, from the perspective of values it can suggest that empirical verifiability is the sole way that value claims can be put forth and justified.[20] In legal education, students study the legal system and learn that there are assumptions about adversarialism that form the basis for arriving at insights about what is fair and just. Law students learn that only by the lawyer advocating zealously for their client against the presumably zealous advocacy of the opposing counsel is a balance of justice and fairness brought about.[21] This can communicate to the law student that adversarialism is the predominant value for basing competing demands about justice and truth.

These distinctions can get frequently blurred when applied to other social and personal contexts. Business school education is premised on assumptions about the fair market system. Throughout the business school curriculum there is the pervasive understanding about the self-apparent good of the capitalist market economy. Students assume and internalize as good the value assumptions of the market.

The point of each of these examples is not to suggest that any of these value assumptions are bad or flawed, but rather to suggest that there are values that are embedded in education throughout the university curriculum. If education is meant to develop a critical self-understanding in students about self and world then it is essential that the moral values that are transmitted through and permeate the academic disciplines be viewed and raised up for critical scrutiny. It is the role of ethics education across the curriculum to provide that inquiry.

In the Professions

Professional education is meant to train students to engage in the practices of the profession and to give them the skills to become competent practitioners.[22] Part of that training is to introduce students to the values and norms that serve to construct the profession itself. Ethical conflicts abound in the professions and it is the role of educators to give students the necessary skills to resolve the critical ethical issues they will face in their future work. It is difficult to think that one could be well trained in the professions without a conscious understanding of the moral parameters of the profession and a developed view of how the profession fits into a larger social and cultural context. It is the role of ethics across the curriculum to provide a process of inquiry that will allow students the opportunity to examine the value assumptions of the profession and to give them the opportunity to critically appropriate these values in light of their own value constructs.

Ethics and the Idea of Practices

This book advances the hypothesis that successful ethics education is education that engages the lived experience of students and compels them to examine both the theoretical coherence and practical meaning of their moral lives. It proposes that the concept of *practices,* as developed in the work of several contemporary philosophers, including Alasdair MacIntyre, Charles Taylor, Pierre Bourdieu, Todd May, and the social scientist Donald Schön, when used as a primary organizing category, offers a way of constructing a coherent philosophical approach for developing a program in ethics across the academic curriculum.[23]

Ethics education takes place in many forms and the goals for that education will vary depending on the context. The idea of practices provides a conceptual framework for the lived experience of students in a variety of educational contexts to be incorporated into the methodology and the pedagogy of the curriculum. Whether in a general educational context, a liberal arts context, or in a professional setting, the notion of practices asks the learner to consider the very activities in which he/she is engaged or is studying, to examine the notion of the good implicit in those activities, and to develop criteria of adequacy for determining right from wrong action. The idea of practices makes ethics education a necessarily self-involving activity.

The concept of practices has been given its fullest formulation in the work of Alasdair MacIntyre. He defines a practice as:

> Any coherent and complex form of socially established cooperative human activity through which goods internal to that form of activity are realized in the course of trying to achieve those standards of excellence which are appropriate to, and partially definitive of, that form of activity, with the result that human powers to achieve excellence, and human conceptions of the ends and goods involved, are systematically extended.[24]

MacIntyre is clear that not all human activities constitute a practice. "Bricklaying is not a practice, architecture is. Planting turnips is not a practice, farming is."[25] The requirements of a practice are that it must yield internal goods that are constitutive of the activity itself. He distinguishes these from external goods, which are those not intrinsic to the activity itself but conferred as rewards or satisfactions for the performance of the activity. Money, status, and prizes are examples of external goods.

For Todd May, practices are constituted by four particular features: 1) they are goal-directed, that is, they have some aim in view; 2) they are governed by social norms in that there are a set of rules and skills that make for the right performance of a practice; 3) they involve regularities of behavior so that people engaged in the same practice are able to say that they are "doing the same thing" under some reasonable description of their behavior; and 4) they involve the use of language.[26]

The idea of practices necessarily engages the student learner (moral agent) because every individual is engaged in the exercise of some practices. Practices provide the link between learner and theory. The level of engaged learning that ensues from this serves the greater educational purpose of ethics across the curriculum to raise the level of moral consciousness among students and the community of higher learning in general.

The idea of virtue is inextricably linked to the activity of a practice. It is impossible to realize the goods internal to a practice without acquiring the quality of a virtue. For MacIntyre a virtue is "an acquired human quality the possession and exercise of which tends to enable us to achieve those goods which are internal to practices and the lack of which effectively prevents us from achieving any such goods. Virtue gives us the power and the skill to achieve the goods that are realizable in a practice."[27] In making this "turn to virtue" MacIntyre links an ethics of action or doing with an ethics or being or agency. This move is important in ethics education in that it enables the learner to see that the goal of ethics is not simply the development of a reasoned understanding of what constitutes an appropriate norm or good action, but also entails practical reason and norms for an understanding of personhood. Ethics education must be linked to an understanding of human moral agency. The idea of practices links ideas of the good with understandings of the moral self.

To be involved in a practice is to be engaged in an activity that has a distinct set of related actions, which together create a sense of design and purpose, and that define a coherent set of actions committed to the achievement of goals and purposes that constitute the practice as such. Implicit in each practice is a sense of the moral good which provides the standards of excellence that are the desired ends of the activity. To be involved in a practice is to be engaged in a moral endeavor. The standards for judging the adequacy of that moral endeavor rest on the degree to which the authentic moral ends are in the process of being realized.

The concept of practices provides a context and framework for understanding the dynamics of the moral life. In identifying those practices that engage persons in their daily lives, MacIntyre sets forth an understanding of how practices give meaning and coherence to lives. An ethics education that highlights the idea of practices involves a critical reflection on what constitutes a practice, what notions of the good inhere in different practices, what skills are necessary to realize the good, and how individuals might act in accordance with the good. It is a self-involving activity.

This book is based on the assumption that the most effective way of engaging in ethics education is through engaging students in reflecting on the practices that constitute their own lives, and the lives they observe and study, and to lead them to understand the way that the practices of their lives and of the world in which they live approximate the moral excellences implicit in the practices themselves. One of the primary goals of ethics education is the development of moral consciousness on the part of students. To develop this it is necessary for students not only to be aware of the moral significance and meaning of their own actions but also to understand how moral arguments are constructed and justified.

Notes

1. Some examples of popular bestsellers include *Ethics for the New Millennium*, by the Dalai Lama (New York: Riverhead Books, 1999) and *The Book of Virtues*, by William Bennett (New York: Touchstone Books, 1996).

2. The allegory of the cave is perhaps the paradigmatic example here. See 514a-521b of Plato's *Republic*.

3. Aristotle's idea of knowing is found in *Nicomachean Ethics*, particularly in book 6. My development of these ideas derives from William Sullivan's *Reconstructing Public Philosophy* (Berkeley: University of California Press, 1982), 66-69.

4. These voices can be heard largely from representatives of the business and corporate communities who contend that American secondary schools and colleges fail to produce graduates with the skills necessary to perform essential jobs for our present and future economy.

5. The idea of appropriation of knowledge and the construction of meaning is taken from the work of Bernard Lonergan. See *Method in Theology* (New York: Herder and Herder, 1972) and *Insight* (San Francisco: Harper and Row, 1978).

6. Paulo Freire, *Pedagogy of the Oppressed* (New York: Seabury Press, 1970).

7. Henry Rosovsky, *The University: An Owner's Manual* (New York: W.W. Norton & Company, 1990).

8. José Ortega y Gasset, *Mission of the University* (London: Kegan Paul, Trench, Trubner, 1946), as cited in Rosovsky, 100.

9. This definition is taken from the work of Charles McCoy. See *Management of Values: The Ethical Difference in Corporate Policy and Performance* (Boston: Pitman Publishing, 1985).

10. For a development of a phenomenological approach to religious ethics, see Howard Harrod, *The Human Center: Moral Agency in the Social World* (Philadelphia: Fortress Press, 1981).

11. The idea of adequacy as a criterion for making normative judgments is developed in the work of David Tracy. See in particular *Blessed Rage for Order* (New York: Seabury Press, 1975).

12. This idea is developed in Francis A. Eigo, ed., *The Professions in Ethical Context: Vocations to Justice and Love* (Villanova, PA: Villanova University Press, 1986), and in William May, *The Physician's Covenant: Images of the Healer in Medical Ethics* (Philadelphia: Westminster Press, 1983).

13. The analysis that follows is drawn from the Teaching of Ethics Project at the Hastings Center. In particular, see Bernard Rosen's *Ethics in the Undergraduate Curriculum*, The Teaching of Ethics IX (New York: Institute of Society, Ethics and the Life Sciences, 1980).

14. Rosen, *Ethics in the Undergraduate Curriculum*, 12.

15. Rosen, *Ethics in the Undergraduate Curriculum*, 13.

16. The relation between the descriptive and normative dimensions of ethics is developed more fully in chapter 2.

17. The classic text on values clarification is the popular *Values Clarification: A Handbook of Practical Strategies for Teachers and Students*, by Sidney B. Simon, Leland W. Howe, and Howard Kirschenbaum (New York: Hart Publishing Company, 1972).

18. This issue is focused on the central question about whether it is possible to teach ethics, and if so, what methods are appropriate for such education.

19. For a comprehensive analysis of the idea of catechesis in religious education see Thomas Groome, *Christian Religious Education: Sharing Our Story and Vision* (San Francisco: Harper and Row, 1980).

20. The analysis of verifiability, objectivity, and the advancement of truth claims developed here is based on the work of Michael Polanyi. See *The Tacit Dimension* (Gloucester: Peter Smith, 1983) and *Personal Knowledge: Toward a Post-Critical Philosophy* (Chicago: University of Chicago Press, 1958).

21. The idea of the attorney as zealous advocate for the client is a pivotal notion in the literature in legal ethics. See David Luban, *Lawyers and Justice* (Princeton, NJ: Princeton University Press, 1988).

22. The literature in professional ethics is abundant. A good summary overview is contained in Eric Mount, Jr., *Professional Ethics in Context: Institutions, Images, and Empathy* (Louisville, KY: Westminster/John Knox Press, 1990).

23. Contemporary treatments of the idea of practices can be found in Alasdair MacIntyre, *After Virtue: A Study in Moral Theory* (Notre Dame, IN: University of Notre Dame Press, 1980); Donald Schön, *The Reflective Practitioner: How Professionals Think in Action* (New York: Basic Books, 1983); Pierre Bourdieu, *The Logic of Practice* (Stanford, CA: Stanford University Press,

1980); Pierre Hadot, *Philosophy as a Way of Life: Spiritual Exercises from Socrates to Foucault* (New York: Blackwell Publishers, 1995); and Todd May, *Our Practices, Our Selves* (University Park: Pennsylvania State University Press, 2001).

24. MacIntyre, *After Virtue*, 175.
25. MacIntyre, *After Virtue*, 175.
26. May, *Our Practices*, 8-15.
27. May, *Our Practices*, 178.

Chapter 2
Introducing Ethics into Every Department: An Overview

"Introducing Ethics into Every Department"? At first glance such a proposition seems rather bizarre and far-reaching. "What is this? A boondoggle for philosophers? What about tap dancing in every department? Tap dancing might, at least, promote the health of the faculty. (Though, come to think of it, senior professors make the most money. Maybe it is in the best interest of the university to scratch tap dancing and offer free cigarettes and booze to the faculty! Then they'd die and we could hire compliant, newly minted Ph.D.'s and save our university a lot of money.)"

I hope the above sounds comical. It *does* poke fun at entrenched attitudes that often face an institution that suggests integrating aspects of a foreign discipline into an established discipline that is doing just fine as it is, thank you. What do we need ethics for? We provide exacting, objective truth to our students that only devotees of our discipline can provide.

These comments point to several perceived problems connected with the hypothesis of integrating the study of ethics into every department in the university. We will confine ourselves in this chapter to three: 1) the fact-value problem; 2) the add-on problem; 3) the comfort-level problem. These three problems will be addressed in order.

1. The Fact-Value Problem

There are, of course, a number of ways to enter into the fact-value problem. Many seek a portal through the social sciences and the natural sciences. In these disciplines a substantial number of practitioners believe that there is a strong fact-value distinction. Let us first explore the basis for this claim and then the arguments against it—concluding with a stance that might move us forward.

First, let us examine the basis of the problem. We all know that when presented with a situation in which we are confronted with purely subjective criteria we feel uncomfortable. This is because we all seek something beyond taste to which we can appeal in order to satisfy our claims.

This is the origin of the inclination in most academic disciplines toward some sort of move toward "objectivity." This is a very understandable move. Socrates in the *Euthyphro* says that the gods agree about objective facts and only argue about subjective issues, such as what pleases them or whether something is just or unjust, beautiful or ugly, good or bad.[1] The meaning of this is simple. All of us feel rather comfortable when confronted with what we believe to be objective criteria. We balk and chafe at purely subjective criteria. We long for the factually objective.

This can be illustrated through examples in three courses of study within the university: English literature (a representative of the humanities), biology (a representative of the natural sciences), and interior design (a representative of a professional/career program).[2]

In English there are some who may be classified as adherents of a critical theory that assumes an objectivity standard. One example of this would include all those who hold the written text up as merely a public artifact that is subject to all the rules of language (another public institution that fixes meaning in a way that can be objectively determined by all).[3] The text, under this theory, may be separated from the author and its historical context because it is an artifact that may be scientifically studied such that all disputes about meaning, etc., could be, in principle, adjudicated. These critics (and they include both the so-called New Critics and the neo-New Critics) hold a version of the objectivity thesis. But why should the audience, author, or societal context be merely opaque? These may each convey values that should be considered when evaluating the significance of a work of art.

Another set of critics also hold to an objective standard. These are the postcolonialists. Many of these adherents set out an objective set of values that affirm a dogma that the dynamic of political imperialism is a fact. Further, this imperialism creates a set of relations that are also factual. These include the artistic elevation of the expressions of the oppressed peoples *simpliciter*.

To some this might be a value-free research design, but it is really dependent upon several enthymemes such as, A1) "All cultural expressions are of equal merit," A2) "The voice of the oppressed is inherently interesting," and A3) "There has been an evil plot (intended overtly or otherwise) that has suppressed the voices of women and oppressed peoples such that much of the best literature in the world has never seen the light of day." There may be merit in these claims or at least in certain aspects of these claims. However, they are often suppressed in the discussion. Instead, it is often the case that one moves from the premise "X is a piece of literature that was heralded by civilization Phi" to "X is a piece of literature that stands on par with Chaucer, Shakespeare, and Milton." This is because Chaucer, Shakespeare, and Milton are heralded by the Anglo-American Culture. And since all cultures are of equal value, then what is valued by any culture is of equal weight to any other.

This argument (or ones like it) occurs regularly in literature departments across America. The burden of proof is to demonstrate that some novel, story, or poem (from the oppressed group) is *not* a purveyor of truth and beauty. But though one may be a member of a group that has been unjustly oppressed, why is it the case that the witness to such per se is excellent art? It may be, but need it necessarily be? The answer to such a question cannot be answered entirely in the objective realm. One must confront these unacknowledged value statements that are added by practitioners and make them a part of the "grand conversation."[4] Unless we do so, we have not captured the complete dynamics of the argument.

In biology (and to some extent science in general), there is a portrayal of knowledge as being out "in nature" for all to examine and understand. Many courses are taught from textbooks with the attitude "Here is established fact. Memorize it." However, this does not give ample expression to the diversity that exists within biology itself, nor to the tradition in the history of science that takes "established fact" and stands it on its head in regular intervals. If all were only fact, and if fact were capable of being understood by clever people, then this shouldn't happen.

What about the direction of science? Does it march in a straight, objective line of ever increasingly accurate visions of the Truth? What about the possibility that scientific research often follows the funding of basic research that is itself often a function of social and political forces within a country (i.e., is value-laden). All of this moves us away from the purely factual objectivity that those textbooks connote.

There is also the myriad of questions of how to use the various discoveries in science. There is far more to science than the machinations of technocrats. One need only turn to the emerging field of genetic engineering to get a glimpse of some of this.[5]

These teasing questions are meant to illustrate that there may be more to biology and science than merely memorizing all of those boldfaced words in the textbooks and perfecting lab technique. Values enter into what we study, how we study it, and what we do with the results once they are published.

Finally is the example of interior design. Interior design is a field that has emerged from interior decorating to encompass many of the functions that an architect might consider respecting the ordering of spaces within buildings.[6] To some, a question of how to organize space effectively is an objective question that makes use of much research from psychologists and human factors engineers. There is a body of data on the effect of colors, carpet, and ergonomic devices that make for an effective workplace.

Many practitioners might think that the only values involved are those of artistic taste: "Do you like blue-gray or the steel-gray colored cubicles? Both have equal mood efficiency scores."

For such interior designers the universe is an objective one with only the occasional intrusion of taste at intersections in which factual test data are equivalent. However, this need not always be the case. In a case that we devised for an interior designer we asked, "Pretend that you are asked to design an entire floor for a service industry company that has a labor intensive operation. It is a very big job for your firm and you have already put a good deal of time into your preliminary study. Now, assume the standard ergonomic size for cubicles is x square feet. Your client tells you that he wants his cubicles $x/2$ square feet. His argument is that he wants to pack twice the people into his space in order to save money (by both renting less office space and being able to supervise their work with fewer supervisors, due to the decreased space the supervisors will have to cover).

You reply that to work in a cubicle of $x/2$ square feet will decrease efficiency due to the ABC study on cubicle size and work output. He responds that he can make his people work with tight supervision.

You think about this and upon reflection believe that to work in a space of $x/2$ square feet would be dehumanizing. You, as interior designer, would be part of a process that created a workspace filled with workers who were treated as just another piece of machinery. You would be an accomplice to creating a workplace that made people feel bad about themselves and very unhappy in their work experience. This result is very wrong. And you will be a part of bringing this evil about. Can you live with that on your conscience?

When you raise these concerns to your client, he laughs. "What do you want me to do, play the violin and cry? Look, it's my money and my company. I have a job that I will have completed *my* way—if not by you, then by someone else."

He has a point. If you pull out, he'll still get the job done and you will be out of a nice fee (one you can really use right now). The point of this example is to illustrate how values can enter even into the professions. If these intersections of value are ignored, are we really educating our students to be effective interior designers?

Those who hold the sharp fact-value dichotomy are committed to creating distinct objective and subjective poles. But do these poles so neatly segregate? Certainly there have been champions of a sharp distinction between objective and subjective statements. These champions approach the problem in different ways. One of the most persuasive of these writers was Rudolph Carnap.[7] Carnap believed that individuals could observe the world via sensory experience in a more or less objective fashion. Sure, it might be the case that some people were color-blind or could not hear some sound because their hearing was not sufficiently acute, but these problems could be handled via an ample sample space and inter-subjective reports about their experience.

From these raw, naive empirical reports, various reliable observation sentences could be constructed that were accurate (according to the operational method of naive reports constrained by intersubjective boundary conditions). These observation sentences could be linked via Ramsey transformation sentences into a form that could be generalized via a mechanical and clearly visible process of induction. For Carnap, the process of induction was not a "power of the soul" as it had been for Aristotle and (to a lesser extent) Mill, but instead was a public and demonstrative exercise in calculation.[8] The result of various acts of induction is to undergo a meta-induction to create a theory that covers all the generalizations in a causal, mechanical structure that reveals the deep symmetry that is assumed to exist in nature.

The result of meta-induction is a theory that can be systematized and presented in an axiomatic order of presentation. In this way, the newly constructed theory tells us something about the world (i.e., is a synthetic proposition[9]) with little to no subjective input. Thus we have discovered and presented objective truth.

This is a powerful presentation. Its advantages are numerous. First, if the presentation is totally correct, then the largely speculative discipline of metaphysics (that aspires to tell us the members of the class of the things that *are* and how those members are related to one another) is rendered superfluous. This is because the things-that-are *are* simply those

things that naive empiricism (as modified by the intersubjective boundary condition) confirms to be. Their *relationships* are dictated by meta-
induction, viz., the theories of science.

Since the things-that-are and their relationships can be demonstrated
without recourse to abstract speculation (subjective flights of fancy),
there is no longer any need for traditional metaphysics. This is heady
stuff. Metaphysics has, since Plato, Aristotle, and the Stoics, been a primary branch of philosophy. If all those questions can be answered by this
simplified, epistemological depiction of philosophy of science, then
epistemology and logic become the most respected areas of philosophy
for they can do all the work.[10] Metaphysics can be dispensed with. The
ontological realm becomes rather tidy and uncluttered. There is (under
this assumption) only one sort of thing: material objects capable of empirical inspection directly (in a foundational sense) or indirectly (via in-
struments that are themselves mediately confirmed by direct observation). All material objects are of equal status (due to the principles of
conservation of matter and of energy) so that cosmology becomes merely
a province of physics that will create mathematical formulae that seek to
explain causation from the beginning and to unite the forces of the universe such as gravitation, electromagnetism, and strong and weak molecular forces.[11]

This positive picture of objectivity is held up as an ideal for many disciplines within the university—not just the hard sciences, but also the
social sciences and many disciplines in the humanities (as we have seen
above). The vision promises that the whims and caprices of subjectivity
can be cleansed from the discipline itself. In its place would be pure objectivity that would carry the weight of truth.

Ah, if only such a picture *could* be true! The critics of the objective
model have (at the very least) raised some challenging difficulties for
this model.[12] From logical difficulties to the inevitable role of the subject
in theory formation to an examination of social influences (including
cultural and political considerations), there are many possible difficulties
to the pure objectivity model.

If even some of these problems are correct, then the objective model is
in serious jeopardy. As much as many of us might wish it would work,
there is the very strong possibility that a better epistemological model is
one that incorporates historical situation and sociological considerations
and the personal worldview of the practitioner.

This is not to suggest that all truth is relative. The purely subjective is
also unacceptable. This is because despite the problems that can arise
with the objective model, still it is not within our power to alter the boil-

ing point of water at sea level. Try as we might, we cannot levitate a brick. There are brute facts outside of ourselves. Thus, the task of epistemology is to offer accounts of how we are to balance clear subjective-interpretative input with this brute other.

Just how this should be done is beyond the scope of this essay, however; what is clear is that the ideal of the purely objective, valueless world should not be presented in our classrooms as the only accepted model. Rather, models that incorporate the values that arise from the subject's interpreting the world and matching it to the common body of knowledge[13] from within his community should be taught, as well.

This means that any synthetic[14] discipline (i.e., one that seeks to describe facts about the world) must incorporate at least some of the subjective (and its ensuing supporting value structure). When values occur they point evaluatively to what should or should not be the case and what is better or worse. When these values connect with human action, then they are issues of ethics. When they do not, they form the axiological background for the discipline. In either case, the values should be studied. In the former case because all the disciplines and professional programs exist within the human community and should consider how they affect the core values of the community. In the latter case because other values (besides ethical values) are also important for authentic mastery of a discipline. (More on this later.)

2. The Add-on Problem

The add-on problem works like this. Professor C believes that she is a good teacher because she has effectively put a lot of important material into her courses. Her classes are so full that she cannot fit another thing in unless she takes something else out. Now, here we have this proposal to integrate ethics and other values into her course. This means (if she is to follow the proposal) that she will have to eliminate something from her course. If she is a chemistry teacher, then she won't be able to go over (for example) chapter fourteen in the textbook. But other students at comparable colleges and universities go over chapters one through fourteen. Her students won't know as much. This will put them into a competitive disadvantage as they apply to graduate school and medical school. Wouldn't Professor C be hurting her students by integrating ethics and values into her course on chemistry?

Obviously, the source of this problem is the assumption that the only real course material for chemistry is found in those chapters of the textbook. If the argument in the fact-value section of this chapter is correct, then chemistry is more than simply learning facts and acquiring lab techniques. Professor C should not think that ethics and value inquiry is merely an add-on to her teaching. It is a *real part* of the discipline. If her students don't get to chapter fourteen but do acquire a fuller understanding of the whole discipline as situated in its context (including, as it must, values and ethics), then they are not being put at a competitive disadvantage but at a competitive advantage.

It has been my experience that many of the most successful and creative heads of major research labs around the country[15] came to their place from other disciplines. For example, one prominent geneticist that I know has his Ph.D. in chemistry. He told me that coming to genetics from outside the discipline gave him an awareness of structures and values that were invisible to those laboring inside the established system. Much as one has critical insights into the ambience of a city or culture when one comes from outside as a foreigner, so also is there critical understanding of academic disciplines. Thus, one response to the add-on question is to reply that the material you are providing can make your students better scientists by giving them a more global, contextual perspective. A global, contextual perspective allows one to consider divergent research designs that approach a problem in many directions. This is sometimes called "big picture" thinking. Part of the big picture includes other scientific contexts. For example, biology is seen in the context of chemistry, and chemistry is seen in the context of physics. But it is more than that. It also includes values. Should I, as a scientist, pursue all questions with the same vigor? Are there some questions that should be avoided because of the social consequences of their results? Is the scientist compelled to think in terms of helping humankind or helping himself to a Nobel Prize in any way he can? All of these involve values and ethics. They are critical components to global big picture thinking. Such a perspective is a valuable tool for anyone seeking excellence in scientific research.

But there is a deeper answer to this query as well. It goes to the foundation of just what a systematic inquiry actually is. When we think of systematic inquiry it is instructive to use the word "science" in its traditional Latin and ancient Greek sense of an orderly, methodological investigation that seeks exact knowledge. Aristotle begins the second book of the *Posterior Analytics* by asking four questions: 1. *Hoti* (What is the

Fact in its "that-ness"? i.e., how it is that we confront the object); 2. *Dioti* (What is the Reasoned Fact? i.e, the account of our understanding the "that-ness" in just such a way), 3. *Ei esti* (Does the thing exist just as described in questions 1, 2, and 4?), and 4. *Ti esti* (What is the nature of the thing? i.e., an integration of the thing into a larger context that gives contextual meaning to what it is).[16] Let's examine these in reverse order.

When one looks at the context of a thing, then she is saying that an essential part of the meaning of an object is revealed through its relationships. For example, take the phrase "mammalian cloning" as understood by a molecular biologist and a layperson. In the first instance it is an indication of a way to create developmental plasticity in adult cells that before the "Dolly" experiment was impossible to bring about. To a layperson it connotes all sorts of science fiction scenarios on the order of *Jurassic Park*.[17]

What is the *real* account? It depends. If one is solely concerned with the *per se* account, then the molecular biologist gives the best rationale. But if one is concerned with the *per aliud* account (not in the "accidental" sense but in the contextual sense of nature), then the informed layperson's reflections are valuable (inasmuch as they are tethered by physical plausibility, as best we know it).

The third question asks whether some thing exists just as we have described it. This is a very important question. In the cloning debate, many people took Dolly to be a definite sign that everything known about biological relationships was about to drastically change. Immediately, there were visions of people creating carbon copies of themselves. (A perfect solution for the person who has to be in three places at once!)

But this is an incorrect contextualization of what cloning would mean. If there are two genetically identical individuals (such as is found in identical twins), then it is by no means the case that they become interchangeable. This is because biology (genotype) is only one ingredient in creating the phenotype and no two phenotypes (even genetically identical phenotypes) will react to their social environment in the same way. Thus the person that each will become is subject to considerable variability. If this is true, then the lay understanding of cloning as a way to correct scheduling problems is false. (And by extension, many of the other popular concerns about cloning are also fallacious.)

Thus, the third question of "if it is" can be a very important one because it forces the person to look critically back and forth between the object as understood contextually in one form and the object as understood in other possible contexts—giving weight to those contexts that seem most correct at the time. Such a process is inherently subjective. But this only demonstrates that the judgments made are by subjects. Subjects may disagree, but, in principle, one of them is right (or more right) than another.[18]

The second question wants an explanation why it is that the ascribed properties attach themselves in the way they do to the object. When Mendel asked the question of why certain floral characteristics were as they were in just such numerical distributions, he was asking an intermediate question that would prompt a contextual question that would, in turn, loop back and ask if things really acted this way (question 3).

Finally, there is the first question: confronting the "that-ness" of an object. The word "that" in English and in ancient Greek (such as we understand it) refers to an encounter with an individual. For example, I have a date with Sally. The date goes badly. Sally is a very mean-spirited and sarcastic person. Do I conclude that all women are mean-spirited and sarcastic? No. This points to the strength and weakness of the first question. The strength is that it forces the subject to confront the object in a rather naive way both through sensation and through rudimentary reflection. This lends an authenticity to the subject's experience of the object. When one stops his experience of an object at a fairly basic level, then there is certain foundational level of certainty that the object might be (at least perceptually) something very close to one's experience of the object.[19]

But it need not be so limited. As one perceives the object, she is prompted to engage another of the questions (2-4). Each time she does this, she will return to the that-ness of the object—not as a naked perceptual given, as at first, but informed by the input of the new question. This time the that-ness is different. It is the first that-ness enriched by the insights of another question. This, in turn, may create a contradiction of sorts. For example suppose that Gregor Johann Mendel was examining tall and dwarf pea plants. When these were crossed, certain patterns emerged that repeated themselves over and over. From this Mendel came up with the idea of genetic dominance.

The that-ness was achieved in Mendel's becoming expert in seeing the various characteristics of pea plants. But viewing the that-ness alone was not enough. He had to speculate upon a reason that accounted for the that-ness (question 2). One might imagine certain mechanisms that were postulated that were not supported when he returned to the that-ness of the pea plants. If the plants did not exist in their that-ness in just this way (question 3), then this caused him to alter his account (redo 2).

The way he would alter his account had to do with various contextual understandings he had in his mind about horticulture and hybridization (question 4). Since Mendel was a Christian monk, his context would also include the notion that all plants and animals exist in a rational created order that is good. This would mean that his search for an account would be guided by reason and that results might be used to better understand and fulfill the function of nature. By doing these things, Mendel would be acting rightly (ethically and religiously). His work could potentially help others. These are questions of value. If one held a different metaphysical position, one could infer different results and perhaps shun scientific inquiry. Thus, all four questions dialectically interact with each other until some equilibrium is achieved.

The manner in which the above scientific (in the old sense) questions dialectically interact is one depiction of the process of induction. According to the account that has been presented, contextual thinking is an important ingredient to the process of induction. This includes the context of science as well as various other values that shape the worldview of the scientist.

Thus, both the big picture thinking involved in research design and the little picture thinking involved in the process of induction make use of contexts and values. Thus, it is not really a question of adding ethics and value inquiry onto a discipline in such a way that you are depriving your students of important "real" subject matter. Rather, values and ethics are an essential component of all systematic inquiry. We are depriving our students when we leave value out.

3. The Comfort-Level Problem

The last question to be raised in this chapter is the comfort-level problem. Given that there has not been (to date) a general concerted effort to integrate value investigation and ethical inquiry into courses across the curriculum, there are many professors who are uncomfortable discussing ethical issues in their courses. The source of this uneasy feeling can be because a) they believe in the objectivity thesis discussed in the first section of this essay, b) they believe in the add-on position discussed in the preceding section, or c) they have not had adequate exposure to structured ways in order to discuss ethical and value questions. Since (a) and (b) have been addressed in the first two sections of this chapter, comments in this section will be directed toward (c).

There are two ways to approach (c): the first is to discuss various attitudes that may affect the way people view the teaching of ethics and values, and the second is to address methods of faculty development that might address these problems. The latter approach will be reserved for chapter 8. Thus, our purpose here is to address the former list of attitudinal barriers to teaching ethics and values in our classes.

Let us begin our inquiry with the issue of trying to be fair. The concern with "being fair" is a consequence of not wanting to be purveyors of propaganda. There have been many instances in the history of humankind in which universities have been used by totalitarian governments as cenacles of indoctrination rather than protected centers of learning. The very mission of modern teaching in America (and most of the industrialized world) has been to foster unfettered, protected debate on issues of value and ethics. When the teacher steps forward and professes "right" answers to these sorts of questions, then something is seriously wrong.[20]

Under one interpretation of the proper response to this potential problem, professors are to efface themselves and strive to present all sides to the issue in such a way that no one can detect the position that the instructor actually holds. After the instructor does this, the student is free to make her own unfettered choices.

I often describe the above interpretation as the "Walter Cronkite approach" after the famous CBS newscaster who tried to assume such a posture in his reporting of the evening news. Proponents of the Walter Cronkite approach are often holders of the objectivity thesis discussed earlier. They believe that the way to present value questions objectively is to create a rounded presentation that covers all sides. The Walter Cronkite approach is thought to be a remedy for the propaganda problem. This is because since all sides are presented equally with the pros and the cons dutifully listed, no one can claim that the presenter is promoting any favorites.

Certainly, if we were forced to choose between the propaganda approach and the Walter Cronkite approach, we would side with the latter. But the choice need not be so stark. There is a middle ground that is preferable to each extreme. The middle approach is to begin with the Walter Cronkite approach and then segue into an exposition of the professor's own position. The professor's opinion (in this context) is merely one of many and thus becomes less coercive to individual students. The object of presenting the professor's opinion is not to create disciples, but to demonstrate to the students that their instructor (who has thought about such questions for some time) has made a choice among all the available choices. This is not to say that the student must necessarily make the same choice, but merely to demonstrate that thinking rational individuals can and do make decisions on these issues and that it *is* important that they do so.

Without adopting the middle way in the above situation there is the very real danger that the student will become a moral skeptic. She may think something like the following: "Here I am in Western Civilization discussing some of the classic theories of justice. The professor has told us the pros and cons of each side and has always played the devil's advocate in class discussion in order that the other side be presented. It seems to me that there is equal merit and demerit to all the positions. Thus, it doesn't matter what I think. You can't really prove anything. All sides are equally right. Different strokes for different folks!"

Such a response is really rather common among students. It mixes extreme moral relativism with moral skepticism. Certainly the latter position is dangerous because it moves ethics and value theory out of the realm of reason and into the realm of taste, e.g., "Should I wear the blue shirt or the red shirt?" The moral skeptic believes that there are *no* correct answers that can be known. If there are right answers, they are unknowable by humans. Moral relativism is also an unfortunate consequence, but is beyond the scope of this book to discuss.[21]

The middle way is an attempt to steer clear of propaganda. Propaganda is wrong because it views the student merely as a means to further the professor's agenda. No student should be viewed as a means only or as a tool for the professor's personal program. Thus the propaganda approach is wrong.

The middle way also steers clear of the flaws in the Walter Cronkite approach, viz., becoming a moral relativist or a moral skeptic. It presents a balanced presentation of the issues and then inserts the professor's view as one among many to be considered. There is no coercion applied to students to adhere to any particular viewpoint, but only to be able to see the values issues and to be able to present a coherent argument in defense of one position.

However, many professors in the academy are still not comfortable that they can provide a discussion of values along the lines discussed above. This is particularly true when one moves outside the core disciplines of the humanities to other fields in which the objectivity thesis still more or less reigns. For these professors and their students, the university must make a decisive move to insert ethics and values studies across the curriculum.

Notes

1. Plato, *Euthyphro*, 9d.

2. These examples do not attempt to be exhaustive in any way—but merely illustrative of some practitioners who profess a model of pure objectivity for their disciplines/professions.

3. An argument could be made to support some form of this argument by referring to Ludwig Wittgenstein. For example, he begins the *Blue Book* by asking the question, "What is the meaning of a word?" This has often been expanded by commentators to "What is the meaning of a sentence?" One can make the argument that for Wittgenstein *meaning* is determined by use (*Gebrauch*), employment (*Verwendung*), or application (*Anwendung*). Meaning is seen in the context of the rules of the language game and those rules, by themselves, "hang in the air." They become rooted only in actual cases. This creates a public basis for meaning. For more on this see Ludwig Wittgenstein, *The Blue and Brown Books* (New York: HarperCollins, 1986), section 1 and *Philosophical Investigations*, 3rd ed. G.E.M. Anscombe, trans. (New York: Macmillan, 1971), section 198.

4. Some of the dynamics of the interactions between oppressors and the oppressed are discussed by Michael Boylan in his article "The Future of Affirmative Action," *Journal of Social Philosophy* 33.1 (September 2002): 117-30.

5. This is obviously an emerging field. One attempt at setting out the science and the values can be found in Michael Boylan and Kevin Brown, *Genetic Engineering* (Upper Saddle River, NJ: Prentice Hall, 2002)—see especially part 3.

6. Much of the information on Interior Design we owe to the Interior Design participants in our Faculty Ethics Seminar (Marymount University 1996-2000).

7. In this depiction I am following Rudolph Carnap's *The Philosophical Foundations of Physics* (Chicago: University of Chicago Press, 1951). There are others who are in sympathy with the results of Carnap but go about the process differently such as Hans Reichenbach, *Experience and Prediction* (Chicago: University of Chicago Press, 1938), and from the point of view of sociology, Max Weber, "Value-Judgments in Social Science," in *Weber: Selections in Translation*, ed. W. G. Runciman (New York: Cambridge University Press, 1978), 69-88. Others, such as Carl Hempel, "Studies in the Logic of Confirmation, Parts I and II," *Mind* 54 (1945): 1-26; 97-121, and Nelson Goodman, *Fact, Fiction, and Forecast* (Cambridge, MA: Harvard University Press, 1954), especially chapters 3 and 4, which point to difficulties in the given formulations, though they share the spirit of the effort.

8. See Rudolph Carnap, *The Logical Foundations of Probability* (Chicago: University of Chicago Press, 1950), especially sections 1-6, and compare to John Stuart Mill, *A System of Logic* (London: Parker, 1843), book 3, chapters 8-10, and Aristotle, *Posterior Analytics* 2.19. Though Mill is somewhat more me-

chanical than Aristotle offering his so-called methods, still there is the gap of recognition. It is this gap that Carnap aspires to bridge.

9. I am using analytic and synthetic in their Kantian interpretations for this passage. This is also the way that Willard Quine interpreted Carnap. See Willard Quine, "Two Dogmas of Empiricism," in *From a Logical Point of View* (Cambridge, MA: Harvard University Press, 1953).

10. For the moment, ethics has been left in the breeze. But some, caught up in the collateral fallout of this movement attempted to create an ethics that would be consonant with many of the positivist principles. These include Stephen Toulman, *Reason in Ethics* (Cambridge: Cambridge University Press, 1950), Charles L. Stevenson, *Ethics and Language* (New Haven, CT: Yale University Press, 1944), and R.M. Hare, *The Language of Morals* (Oxford: Clarendon Press, 1952), among others.

11. The grand unification theories of science (GUTS) are projects on the scale of the logical empiricists in the twentieth century. They seek to unify the disparate fields of astrophysics and quantum physics. For a discussion of this debate see *Lattice Gauge Theory, Super Symmetry, and Grand Unification: Proceedings of the 7th Johns Hopkins Workshop on Current Problems in Particle Theory,* ed. G. and Kovesi Damokos, and S. Domokos (River Edge, NJ: World Scientific Publishing Company, 1984) and *Grand Unification: Proceedings of the Conference,* ed. M. Bianchi (River Edge, NJ: World Scientific Publishing Company, 1993).

12. Some of the most prominent of these critics include Thomas S. Kuhn, *The Structure of Scientific Revolutions,* 2nd ed. (Chicago: University of Chicago Press, 1970), Paul Feyerabend, *Against Method* (London: Verso, 1975), and *Realism, Rationalism, and Scientific Method* (Cambridge: Cambridge University Press, 1981). These writers have called into question the dispassionate objectivity in science. Their work owes a debt to Willard Quine who wrestled with finding ways to try and express a give and take developmental process in which the individual and the world interact with each other. In the end Quine's amalgam seeks to emphasize the objective. See "Natural Kinds" in *Ontological Relativity and Other Essays* (New York: Columbia University Press, 1969). Kuhn and Feyerabend, on the other hand, set out an analysis, which emphasizes more strongly the force of the subjective upon the endeavor of science. Like it or not, the subjective influence will be there.

13. By the common body of knowledge I mean that data that tends toward the objective that has been accepted as being true within a given community and within a theoretical tradition as well as the core values of that tradition. For a further discussion of this sense of the common body of knowledge see Michael Boylan, *The Process of Argument* (Englewood Cliffs, NJ: Prentice Hall, 1988), chapter 1.

14. The reader may note that the claim is made in terms of "synthetic disciplines," meaning those whose mission is to demonstrate the properties that may be attributed properly to subjects in a nontautological fashion. This definition does not necessarily apply to "analytic disciplines" that may be governed by some sort of internal coherence theory of truth. I do believe that even here the subjective value-laden variable occurs. This is through the fashioning of the internal rules of the system. These rules are chosen to be one way as opposed to another. By this choice of rules and the conditions of truth, the inventor of the system evinces personal dispositions to one set of procedures over others. This is sort of a second-level subjective input that would require further argumentation to properly document.

15. My personal experience in this instance concerns biological research labs, but I believe the point can be extended to chemistry as well.

16. *Posterior Analytics*, 2.1 (89b, 21-25). Translations and exegesis are mine.

17. For a good example of some of these lay interpretations see Dorothy Nelkin and M. Susan Lindee, "Cloning and the Popular Imagination," *Cambridge Quarterly of Healthcare Ethics* 7.2 (Spring 1998): 145-49.

18. This, of course assumes that there is, in fact, a true realist account of nature that can be expressed (contra the tradition of Heracleitus and Lao-Tzu).

19. Again, there are a number of foundational, realist assumptions that have been suppressed in this simplified depiction.

20. It should be noted that some philosophers, namely the emotivists, would not have a problem with relegating ethics to nonrational means that amount to propaganda. This is because ethics can aspire to no more. For a presentation of this position see C.L. Stevenson, *Ethics and Language* (New Haven, CT: Yale University Press, 1944).

21. For an introduction to some of the principal issues involved in moral relativism see Michael Boylan, *Basic Ethics* (Upper Saddle River, NJ: Prentice Hall, 2000), 8-13; see also Kai Nielson, "Egoism and Relativism" in *Perspectives in Philosophy,* ed. Michael Boylan (New York: Harcourt Brace, 1993), 1-9.

Chapter 3
The Use of Narrative and Character in Ethics across the Curriculum

Every student who enters the classrooms of our colleges and universities already has a set of values, moral outlooks, and ethical standards that shape his or her behavior and moral decisions. These moral worldviews originate from a variety of sources—from parents, religious and ethnic communities, from churches, synagogues, and mosques, from the culture of which they are a part. If ethics education across the curriculum is to be effective it must take into account these preexisting frameworks and address both their content and substance in order to allow students the ability to critically assess their own ethical standards and appropriate an original and authentic set of ethical insights. This is best done by focusing on the method by which morality is developed in individuals and groups and by providing a framework and process that allow students the ability to understand their own moral growth and development. The idea of narrative as a form of practice provides an especially effective category for this type of reflection and learning process.

The resurgence of interest in a focus on an ethics of character and virtue has brought with it a renewed appreciation for the role that stories and narratives play in the formation of the moral self. We are all products of stories. From the moment we were able to listen to those around us, elders as well as peers, we have been the hearers of stories. We learn about the activities of those who came before us, and of other lands, times, and peoples, as we learn to develop our imaginative capacities for contextualizing our own experience, time, and location. Stories are at the heart of our self-understanding and so they are crucial to the construal of our moral lives. Since the content of virtue and character emerges from an understanding of the cultural and historical narratives of communities and selves, the telling of stories and the determining of a story's authenticity and truthfulness are both essential and helpful for developing an adequate understanding of the moral life. For this reason, a focus on narrative provides a useful method for organizing ethical reflection in the classroom context. This chapter will assess the salient issues in an understanding of the ethics of character, narrative, and virtue and show how these are relevant to the concrete practice of teaching ethics, through a case study.

One of the most trenchant critiques of the ethics of character is that it fails to provide normative criteria by which to make concrete ethical decisions.[1] This chapter attempts to address this issue by providing some of these criteria. Its basic contention is that there are identifiable components, which I will call essential values, that are constitutive of and necessarily entailed by the concept of character, and that these values can be articulated as formal, processive norms that provide guidance for making moral decisions in applied settings.

I will develop this claim in both a theoretical and practical way in three parts. I will first provide an overview of what I understand to be the main claims that are advanced by contemporary proponents of an ethics of virtue and character, as well as an assessment of the contributions and weaknesses of this approach. This overview and analysis are necessary in that I will contend that the limits and possibilities of virtue ethics in the context of ethics across the curriculum parallel the limits and possibilities of the ethics of character in general. Part II will offer a constructive analysis and proposal for the use of a virtue ethic by delineating what the literature in the ethics of virtue proposes are essential ingredients to moral experience. Here I will argue that these components take the form of constitutive values, which can be cast in the form of norms, and that these provide a necessary complement to character ethics. These values and norms counter the criticism that character ethics provides no normative guidance for decision making. In part III, I will explore how these norms provide direction and guidance in the teaching of ethics across the curriculum. I will use a case study, which I will draw from my own teaching experience, and which I take to be representative of the kind of ethical dilemmas that face many professors today. My purpose in exploring this case is not to engage in a detailed analysis of its specifics but to explore in a general way how a virtue or narrative approach to ethics might be used to help resolve complex practical moral dilemmas in a classroom setting.

I. The Ethics of Character: An Overview

While certainly character is a classical notion that is central to the ethical theories of Aristotle, Augustine, and Aquinas, its newfound popularity in theological and philosophical circles is attributable chiefly to the works of writers like Alasdair MacIntyre, Stanley Hauerwas, James McClendon, Gilbert Meilaender, Terrence Tilley, and others. The dominant impulse behind the surge in interest in character ethics was and continues to be a dissatisfaction with much of "the standard account of ethics," that is, among other things, an interminable search for the foundations of ethics, an almost exclusive reliance on norms and principles to direct moral action, an excessive focus on "decisions" and "actions" as the primary form of moral analysis, and a failure of moral theory to sufficiently account for the way that moral decisions are patterned together in a unity within the moral self.[2] The resurrection of character and virtue are seen as remedies to these deficiencies.

For those who are concerned with ethics across the curriculum, the use of the concept of character offers great promise for moral insight and guidance. I am in basic agreement with the proponents of a virtue ethic that looking at moral problems through the lens of character opens up a horizon of insight and also a framework for moral analysis that is unavailable when ethics is seen as simply a search for and the application of the correct moral principles. In particular, the moral psychology provided by a virtue ethic is rich in its capacity to capture the nuances and subtleties of moral phenomenology. At the same time however, I am critical of many of the contemporary attempts to develop an ethics of character. The reasons for my criticisms will become clear in the course of this analysis.

Two works serve as examples of attempts to apply the insights of a virtue ethic to the realm of applied ethics. Oliver Williams and John Houck's 1978 book *Full Value* demonstrated how the use of stories, and in particular the stories of the Jewish and Christian traditions and the master images presented in these stories, can serve to guide moral actions and help individuals apply the insights of their religious tradition to practical business decisions.[3] While developing an important insight into the relevance of character ethics and story to the business world, the book is ultimately unsuccessful due to its failure to be sufficiently precise about the thorny epistemological and theological problems that arise in appropriating virtues and stories in practical settings.

A much more successful effort can be found in Thomas L. Shaffer's *Faith and the Professions*.[4] Shaffer shows a keen sense of the ways that stories and character have concrete application in the professions and particularly in the way that the professions function in American life. Again, however, Shaffer is not entirely successful in that he is unable to spell out with precision exactly how stories influence, shape, and lead to moral choice. He shows that stories can influence choices but not how they do. Both of these works are to be applauded for developing an important insight. A narrative approach to ethics education attempts to follow the insight that there is an important link between character, narrative, and moral choice. And yet the works mentioned are unsuccessful in that they fail to spell out how one moves from virtue to action to help in enabling decision makers to make practical moral choices. It is to this general set of issues surrounding character ethics that we must turn to see how the virtue approach can help those with practical needs.

Virtue, Character, and Narrative: The Major Claims

The ethics of character does not refer to a monolithic body of literature in either classical or contemporary philosophy or theology. Indeed, there are several divergent strands of ethical discourse that can be broadly classified as virtue ethics. My proposal here is that it is possible to identify certain essential elements in the contemporary literature on virtue and that these elements constitute a cluster of central claims that are representative of a virtue approach to ethics. These commonly accepted insights can provide a basic departure point for understanding how virtue can be used in educational contexts.

1) There is a *deficiency in the standard account of ethics* in that it focuses excessively on either quandaries, decisions, actions, or principles that tend to be seen as distinct and separate from one another.[5] In each of these modes moral discourse can become the "ethics of the big event," collapse into a type of rote and rationalistic legalism, or be "reductionistic" in that it fails to capture the fullness of moral experience.[6]

2) A retrieval of *the notion of character* in ethics focuses attention on those moral qualities of the self that orient or dispose a person to the good. Character particularizes a distinct moral identity and connotes the way that particular virtues are ordered together within the self or a community in a distinctive way. Character refers to the unity, coherence, and integration of the self as the way that the self (or the group or community) is oriented to moral excellence and the good.[7]

3) *Virtues* are those qualities that are intrinsic to a person or community that either enable them to achieve a particular end (telos), qualities that enable individuals to perform their social roles, or qualities that enable one to achieve worldly or social success (utility). Virtue is "an acquired human quality the possession and exercise of which tends to enable us to achieve those goods which are internal to practices and the lack of which effectively prevents us from achieving any such goods."[8]

4) The virtues, values, norms, and principles that constitute one's character derive from basic fundamental *convictions* about what is considered true, right, and good. These virtues and standards are given content only as they are perceived as deriving from a foundational self-identity that is the result of a particular history (of the self or community) over time.[9] The meaning and content of these *virtues are contained in the stories and narrative traditions of particular communities*. The telling of stories, the articulating of the images and metaphors that guide self-understanding thus become essential for making adequate moral judgments and choices.

5) To have character and possess *vision* in a moral sense means that one's moral outlooks and perceptions are shaped by the kinds of stories that constitute the essence of a particular community's tradition. Moral vision, the way that one sees the moral world and the capacity that one has for seeing, will therefore be a central element in ethical discourse. This implies that an aesthetic mode of analysis will be of central concern for ethical discourse.[10]

6) *Practices* are those activities that are internal to a person's or community's tradition, which provide the means or form of activity by which virtue will be realized within that tradition. Therefore, an explication of the practices of a community will be central to moral analysis.[11]

7) Stories, virtues, and practices all constitute the tradition of a particular person or community. The moral rules and laws of a community are also part of that tradition. Essential to moral discourse will be those aspects of *a moral tradition* that provide the substantive forms of the tradition itself.[12]

Character Ethics: The Major Contributions

The retrieval of character ethics has been a most welcome addition to contemporary ethical discourse. While its contributions have been many, there are several features that I deem to be the most significant:

1) A virtue ethic widens the scope of moral analysis. It represents what is referred to as "the turn to the subject." In that character ethics has focused attention away from acts isolated from one another and onto the way that actions are connected and patterned together into some unity (as suggested by the ideas of character and story), a reductionistic understanding of the moral life as being a matter of the search for irreducible foundations or the application of moral principles to problems has been corrected. Casuistry has been the dominant form of the moral methodol-

ogy (particularly in Roman Catholic ethics) and character ethics offers an important "widening" of the way that the scope and task of ethics is construed.[13]

2) A virtue ethic offers a rich theory of the moral self. Because character implies a unity and integration, there is an impulse in character ethics to include the multifaceted aspects of the way that the moral self is constituted in moral analysis. While much of post-Enlightenment ethics (Kantian, natural law, utilitarian) tends to emphasize the rationalistic and logical properties of the moral self, character ethics pushes to see the self as a whole, encompassing not just the rational qualities of agency, but also the role of imagination, the aesthetic, the role of vision, and of affectivity. The moral self is one that not only calculates and rationalizes but also understands and knows by comprehending aesthetic beauty and the emotional dimensions of human experience.

3) Character ethics through the use of the concept of narrative also helps to account for the idea of development and change within the moral life. Narrative and character, in that they imply the ongoing communication and connection of ideas and events over time, suggests that the moral self and the moral tradition are in the process of continual transformation. This presents a challenge to some forms of ethical discourse that are premised on a static view of the human person and of the moral community.[14]

4) An ethics of narrative provides a way in which the norms and principles that constitute a moral tradition can derive their substance and meaning. Stories make principles come alive. For example, within the Christian tradition the norm of love as agape is central. The content of this norm is given meaning only when it is given substance by the stories of the person of Jesus and the various stories of the Christian community in which agape is lived out.[15]

5) The use of character and story in ethics has given rise to the use of biography and autobiography as important and vital ways of gaining moral insight. By looking at the way that saints, heroes, and ordinary folk "put together a moral life over time" it becomes possible to derive moral insight about how the moral life can and should be lived. This approach avoids the reductionism of some ethics and shows how ethic's proper domain involves making choices continually about how one perceives the moral good to be acting in one's life and discovers a path that leads to the realization of virtue and character (the good) over time. Ethics in this light becomes a question of "becoming a type of person" rather than focusing explicitly on doing or performing certain actions.

Character Ethics: Its Major Flaws and Weaknesses

The criticisms of character ethics have been serious ones, and ones which go to the heart of the enterprise of ethics in general. I take the most compelling criticisms to be the following:

1) The contention is made that while character is indeed an interesting lens from which to view morality, at its basis morality is constituted by moral choice and it is only through action and the observance of laws and rules that moral activity takes place. If character ethics is characterized as an ethics of being, and an ethics of norms and principles seen as an ethics of doing, the contention of the ethics of character that being is prior to doing is flawed in that being is only manifested by doing. It is important to see, critics of character ethics claim, that being and doing are integral parts of the same reality. Character is formed by the action that persons perform and virtues are given content by how they are manifested in people's actions. The virtue/obligation debate tends to have an either/or caste to it. The critics of character ethics contend that the dispositions of character are perhaps premoral categories and are not constitutive of actual morality.[16]

2) The actual way that stories affect moral judgments is problematic. Proponents of character ethics see stories as essential to moral choice. While it is clear that stories do in fact influence outlooks and moral choices, it is unclear in most treatments of character however *exactly how* stories serve to affect our moral judgments. In most developments of the idea of story in ethics, the end result is a juxtaposition of story and moral choice. This can be seen particularly in works such as Thomas Groome's *Christian Religious Education*[17] and Gilbert Meilaender's *The Limits of Love.*[18] The intrinsic link between these two is not sufficiently developed in the literature.[19]

It is unclear in exactly what ways stories are normative. Do they instruct by intuition? Do they offer concrete guidelines for action? Are moral principles transposed from story to action?

3) Most treatments of character ethics have developed virtue and story along individualistic lines.[20] In other words, to speak of character has meant to speak of an individual's character rather than to speak of the character of groups, institutions, and structures. While some attention has been paid to addressing a community's character, little has been paid to how institutions and collectivities within a community can be said to have character. Particularly lacking in the literature on character ethics is a concern for the structural components of group action. A general lack

of awareness of the contributions of social science exists in the current literature.[21]

4) The use of narrative in theology and ethics, despite what its proponents claim, has tended to take a sectarian cast. In other words, the stories of a given community serve to inform the moral life of the community but it is unclear whether or in what ways the moral insights of a given community have moral authority beyond the boundaries of that particular community. Is there a basis for a public ethic on the terms of an ethics of character? Is a particular community's ethic relative to the ethic of another community?[22]

5) There is imprecision in the way that criteria are developed for the justification and truthfulness of stories within an ethics of narrative. There is a circularity to the idea of truth within a story-dependent ethic (the moral authority for the truth of a story is contained within the story itself). More attention needs to be paid to how criteria of truthfulness and justification are developed within an ethics of narrative.[23]

6) The foundationalism vs. nonfoundationalism debate casts a shadow on the ethics of character. Issues of ethical pluralism, the debate about the rational or other foundations of an ethic, the possibility of cross-cultural ethics all need to be addressed by those who propose an ethics of virtue and character.[24]

While each of these issues raises some question about the completeness with which an ethic of virtue can be utilized in moral discourse, my contention is that the idea of virtue constitutes a necessary component of a comprehensive ethic. Moreover, this chapter contends that there are formal processive norms that are necessary components of a virtue ethic, which give virtue a normative framework that provides a basis for making moral decisions.

II. Ethical Principles and Character Ethics

An exploration of each of the component parts of an ethic of virtue suggests that some essential values or components are entailed by the very nature of character and narrative and that these values can be formulated as formal norms that give direction to how that value (component part) is to be realized and actualized. These norms function morally in that they provide a framework of action-guides, which decision makers must necessarily consider to get normative guidance throughout the decision-making process. Each of the criteria in and of themselves is insufficient to ground adequately a moral decision but together these norms form a constellation of moral points that serves to direct, focus, and clarify the moral choices with which one is faced.

1. *Consistency.* To say that someone has character is to infer that the individual possesses certain virtues that orient him / her toward the good. To be virtuous means that one can be counted on to act in distinctive ways, that one has developed the habit of acting in certain ways in distinction from other possible ways, that one is identified as acting in a way appropriate to and consistent with the distinguishing feature that marks one's character (to be loving, to be faithful, to be loyal, etc.). It is the distinctive way that virtues are situated and embodied in the self that identifies character.

To have character and to be virtuous means that one acts consistently with the virtues that one has developed. Consistency is one way of describing habitual action. In this light then consistency can be said to be a norm that is requisite to virtue. In terms of concrete decision making this suggests that an essential question to ask of a particular decision or choice would be whether this choice is consistent with the types of actions for which a person or an institution has become known.

2. *Coherence.* Character is a term that connotes the unity of the moral self in a distinctive and particular way. Character implies that there is an integration and unity within the self and that the differing parts of the moral personality are related to one another in some integrated way. The different experiences of the past and present find their meaning within the household of the self. This meaning is contained in and communicated through the narratives of the self and the community that form the content of one's tradition. Narratives convey the connections between events and relate experiences by threading them together in a type of patterned unity or narrative structure. Events take on meaning and intelligibility when they fit within the framework of a community's or person's narrative. This framework might be articulated in the themes, myths, or images by which a community identifies itself. Both character and narrative therefore are marked by their achievement of coherence—events "hang together in some unified way."

Moral choices and decisions are "parts" which fit into some larger unity or whole. The part-whole structure, as well as the idea of the fitting, are important dimensions of moral and theological analysis that can be found most explicitly in the works of H. Richard Niebuhr and James Gustafson.[25] It is important therefore to ask in the decision-making process whether an action or a decision actually fits into a larger sense of purpose and meaning. It is necessary to ascertain how one decision is related to other decisions of the moral agent. In institutions, for example, coherence suggests that the parts of the organization need to be coordinated to the extent that actions across the institution are not self-contradictory. A vital question to explore is whether the moral entity as a whole represents a unified and integrated decision-making structure. The norm of coherence requires a search for interconnectedness and unity.

The use of the metaphor of organism is helpful for understanding the function of coherence in ethical decision making.[26] If the moral self or the moral community is to be coherent there must be a relationship between the parts and the whole. In an organism each of the parts must contribute to the effective functioning of the organism as a whole. When there is a deficiency in the parts the total entity becomes impaired and dysfunctional.

The foregoing analysis suggests that coherence can be construed in two basic ways: as referring to the way that events connect over a span of time; or as referring to the way that decisions relate to other parts of the moral agent (i.e., how one department of an organization relates to another department of the same organization). Both of these frames of reference would need to be further developed to attend adequately to the requirements of the norm of coherence in an ethics of character.

3. *Continuity.* To use narrative in ethical decision making means to locate moral choices within the context of a "unified life story." That is, it is to try to assess in what ways a particular choice has some connection to the developing historical story, to show how a choice "flows out of" or "fits into" the history of a person or community. Continuity must be understood here, however, as not merely implying that all moral decisions ought not be disruptive of a community's history. Indeed, some choices are justifiably disruptive.

For all moral choices there needs to be some recognizability as to how a decision is related to the patterns and events of the past and to the future. A decision might be disruptive and yet the disruption would have to have some legitimacy and justification based on the essential canon of the story.[27] Liberation theology can serve as an example. The theme of liberation is central to the biblical narrative of the Jewish and Christian peoples. A decision to live faithful to the theme of liberation however would perhaps be disruptive to the "effective" functioning of the political or social order of the historical self or community. The moral choice however might be said to be morally legitimate in that it is contained in and "continuous with" the "larger" story of the community. In other words, liberation is both a central theme and moral requirement of the Jewish and Christian traditions and can be cited as a legitimating source of moral action.

As a norm the idea of continuity suggests that assessment of a moral decision would explore the ways that the decision would best continue the tradition into the future and that there would have to be some element of recognizability within the tradition for the legitimacy of the choice.

4. *Correction*. A fundamental claim in a narrative approach to ethics is that while there is a basic tendency to the construction of stories that are coherent and continuous, there is at the same time a movement to chaos and discontinuity that are at play in the human drama at all times. It is important then to understand how narratives need to be changed, altered, freshly interpreted, and lived out in ways that may appear to be at odds with the historical patterns of the past.

No story can be assumed to be self-evidently true. Any story can be distorted, wrongly interpreted, used for injurious purposes, or jettisoned for other stories deemed more compelling. The task of an ethics of character is to develop the skills to understand when the destructive dynamics and impulses of a story need to be modified and changed. Developing such skills of moral discernment is one of the essential elements of ethical inquiry and practice. In a narrative approach to ethics these skills are used to assess the adequacy of a story to carry the meaning and value of a tradition into the future.

The implication of this insight is that it is important that critical questions be asked about the stories. It should not be presumed that there is a linear trajectory of a story into a harmonious future but that every story and each interpretation of the story be assessed and reevaluated in light of the present context, times, and demands. Correctives need to be made where there are deficiencies; new insights and actions are required where the demand calls for new responses. The authenticity of each person, community, and institution needs to be claimed and appropriated anew. The process of ethical inquiry requires a reexamination and re-appropriation of existing stories and traditions.

5. *Communication/Conversation*. Narratives can be transmitted in several ways. They can be carried on through spoken or written word. They can be contained in the myths, images, art, and music that explain, guide, and direct a person or a community. They can be contained in propositions and beliefs. Whatever the form of the insights, only communication can transmit the truths of a tradition. This suggests that moral decision making requires communication, or perhaps more aptly a conversation among all the relevant actors in the moral environment in which a decision is being made.[28]

There are various imperatives that would follow from an emphasis on communication. There is the inference that the communication be a truthful communication and that it not be "partial" or "reductionistic"; that is, that the communication be based on the totality of the insights available, be carried on in good faith by those who converse, and that the conversation include all those participants that have a rightful and necessary place in the decision-making process. There needs to be some way to assess the adequacy of the conversation that surrounds moral choice. A theme or norm that emerges in this idea of communication is that of *inclusion* and *comprehensiveness*. Authentic conversation is conversation where there is no self-deception, where all "relevant" aspects of the issue at hand are being considered, and in which all "relevant" actors to the issue are involved in the conversation.

One important concern that arises from the concept of conversation in social ethics is whether the existing structures allow for authentic conversation. Are the structures sufficiently inclusive and comprehensive to prevent self-deluded and reductionistic answers to emerge to pressing moral choices?

6. *Convictions*. While not exactly fitting into the schema as a norm per se, the role of convictions in the decision-making process is essential. Convictions are those beliefs that a person or institution has that identify the person in such a way that to change those convictions would make the person or community a distinctively different person.[29] Convictions are those values and beliefs that serve as the foundation upon which all moral choice derives. They have a priority status in moral discourse. These convictions are usually explicit and are self-consciously articulated although at times they can be quite tacit. In an institutional setting they are embodied in statements of mission and purpose or in a code or credo that is used as a reference point from which to judge organizational actions.

The literature on corporate cultures explores examples of how a set of convictions in professional settings serves to guide an organization's moral (policy) choices.[30] To articulate these convictions as norms would entail requiring decision makers to ask how a decision is related to the convictions of an organization. Does this decision reflect the essential beliefs that go to the core of the identity of this person or group? The norms of consistency and continuity would use convictions as one basis upon which to ground moral choices.

7. *Creativity*. One of the criticisms of the ethics of character is that it cannot readily account for newness and change in the identity and direction of a person or group. The charge is sometimes made that character ethics has a bias to a status quo orientation. Words like consistency, continuity, connection, unity, and integration can be construed as reflecting a

preference for harmony and cohesion over conflict and change. Accounting for the radical demands of the new situation or openness to different directions does not immediately seem to be of central importance for character ethics. While this has been true in some developments of character ethics, there is no necessary reason for this.

Habitual action needs to be distinguished from rote performance. To be virtuous means that one possesses the skill of prudence which enables one to make discerning judgments about the way that the good (God), theologically is manifested and realized in the particulars of a given moment or choice. The writings of Iris Murdoch are instructive in this regard in that she speaks of the moral life as constituted by having the capacity to focus and shift attention on authentic and compelling objects of beauty and good, thus suggesting the aesthetic mode of apprehension as being able to offer moral insight and wisdom.[31] Such an apprehension of the moral good entails being open to having one's perception and vision affected by the revelation of the good in the newness of each moment. In this sense then, there is a radicality in the ethics of character to be open to possibilities of transformation and conversion.[32]

Practically, the requirements of an imperative of creativity suggest that each moral decision needs to be scrutinized as to whether it takes sufficient account of new ideas and discoveries, and whether there is an openness to different ways of looking at issues and problems that challenge our traditional ways of acting and thinking. There is a tendency to stasis in the moral lives of individuals and groups. The ethics of narrative has resources for challenging this stasis.

Using the Principles: The Constellation Theory

Each of the values and norms articulated here is a necessary but not sufficient criterion for moral decision making. The values translate to norms, each of which must be factored into moral analysis in addressing a particular ethical problem. The norms and values can be seen as points that together constitute a constellation that acts as a moral framework. Each point in the constellation must be viewed in reference to the other points. Each will serve to support, counter, challenge, modify, or illumine the other points in the constellation.

Since each part is a component necessary to character and narrative, the norms and values must be taken as a composite whole. The normativity of this framework is realized in the harmonization, correlation, and correction of its component parts, that is, each component must be seen in reference to the other components. This correlation reduces the possibility that moral choices will be the result of myopic or reductionistic outlooks.

What emerges in this configuration is a clarification of our moral vision. We begin to see more clearly the objects of attention that draw us and compel us to moral action. A vision of the moral good emerges in this process, which focuses our attention in ways that heretofore were known only partially or in an obscure or hidden way. This vision incorporates not only virtues and values but also norms that are directive of moral choices.

The central insight of the normativity of this constellation theory functions in a way similar to the idea developed by Charles Curran in his "The Stance of Moral Theology."[33] Curran contends that there are certain truths and value assumptions that constitute the central insights of the Christian tradition, and that these function as a preexisting set of values that premise moral choices in the Christian context. The moral agent, as one schooled in the stories of the Christian tradition, operates with a horizon of consciousness that is constituted by the following beliefs: 1) a basic belief that all *creation* is of God and is good; 2) a belief that *sin* is the condition that limits humans from fully comprehending and realizing the original goodness of creation; 3) a belief that the *Incarnation* is the event in which God's ultimate self-identification with humans is realized and that because of this event we are afforded salvation from the bonds of sin; and 4) a belief that the *Redemption and Resurrection Destiny* of Jesus informs us that only in the future will the fullness of God's kingdom be realized. Curran indicates that a Christian ethic that accentuates any of these to the elimination of or disproportionality to any of the others suffers from a reductionism that is morally inadequate.

The same claim is true of the normative framework developed here, albeit with some differences. While Curran is referring to a preexisting horizon of theological and moral convictions that serves as a departure point for reflection, the constellation theory of an ethics of virtue is given conscious realization in the decision-making process itself. The major claim of the theory is that the values and norms that constitute a moral framework need to be seen as parts of a whole.

An obvious objection to this account is the issue of how conflicts between norms are resolved and how priority among these values and norms is to be determined. These are admitted shortcomings that need to be explored in greater detail in subsequent work. A crucial test of the adequacy of the proposals I have made depends on how these insights serve to help those faced by moral dilemmas make decisions that are constructive of what they know to be good.

III. The Method Applied: A Case Study

Narrative Ethics and Vocational Choices

Over the past fifteen years I have taught a course at Georgetown University to undergraduate seniors on "Ethics and the Professions." Since the course includes undergraduates from a variety of disciplines and with multiple majors, and since seniors are in the midst of making choices about their future, the course focuses on developing a basic understanding of what constitutes a profession and how particular professions reflect different normative worldviews. One of my goals in the course is to engage students in thoughtful reflection about their own professional or career choices and to give them a larger framework and context for their own particular choice of a career direction or path. The major project for the course is the writing of a vocational autobiography. This entails a recounting of the formative events and influences that have shaped each student's view about how he or she intends to pursue his or her own professional or vocational decisions.

The vocational autobiography project typically engages the students in a gripping way. It asks that students tell their own stories—the stories of those events, people, and experiences that have shaped their lives and influenced the formation of their "professional" (vocational) worldview. The assignment then asks the student to critically assess the stories they have been formed by, view them in relation to other possible stories, and develop a justificatory set of explanations that have the ability to be morally convincing and to explain why they should make the kind of vocational choices they intend to make. The project seems initially to be merely a test of developing memory and recounting experiences in a descriptive mode. The task, however, is much more challenging. The moral task is to understand the move from a descriptive to a normative understanding, the move from understanding the facts of the formation process to comprehending the way that there is a normative force and direction to the path of self-identity and consequently to the choices that lead to and create that path.

The constellation theory developed here provides a way of detecting the "normative force" inherent in a past story and projects the story into a necessary and desired future. To develop this one needs a *set of criteria* for what constitutes the normative direction of the story and that can lead one to make the choices necessary to achieve the desired and necessary future. Each of the points of the theory indicates a criterion for assessing one's own vocational decisions.

Consistency. Is this choice consistent with the previous actions for which my community or I have become known? Is it recognizable as an extension of my past, not necessarily in an "unbroken" way, but as reflective of the core values that I hold?

Coherence. Is this choice in line with other choices and decisions that I make in other arenas or departments of my life? Is there integration among my choices such that there is a reasonable relationship and integration of my behaviors such that they do not create a disproportionate rupture or alienation in my psyche or spirit?

Continuity. Is there a reasonable relationship between my career or professional choice and the development and evolution of my own personality and character? Does this choice fit into a larger pattern of choices that define my character when viewed from a larger or more comprehensive perspective?

Correction. Has the story I have internalized thus far about who I am and what I might do in my life provided constructive results? Has it created the kind of person that stands for what I believe to be good and true? What distortions have crept into the story? Is this story premised on lies or unexamined assumptions? What changes need to be made to the story to assure that it is my own authentic story and not merely the story that has been handed on to me by those who have come before? Am I adopting this story merely because it is the easiest and most comfortable one available? What am I called to do and who am I called to be that is different than what I have already done and requires new growth that may perhaps be difficult and challenging?

Communication. Has the process that has led to this decision been one that has been carried on with the appropriate consultation and communication? Have I been in conversation with or sought input from those individuals or sources that are important guides for my own development and sense of placement in the world? Have I sought "alternative" perspectives for my own choices so that they do not represent merely a safe and predictable course of action but have the ability to stretch my own development?

Convictions. Do my career choices reflect the beliefs and values that I hold to be important and reflective of a truthful life? The moral life must derive from a set of convictions about reality that reflect our deepest understandings of a worthwhile life. Are my career choices consistent with those convictions?

Creativity. Do my career choices reflect my own imaginative possibilities for the kind of life that will both contribute to the world's need and provide motivation and inspiration for me in my life's journey? Have I sought to imagine my life in terms of possibility and new expressions rather than in predictable and safe modes? Does this decision take into account new ideas and discoveries that I have examined?

While simply asking these questions creates no assurance of moral consensus or clarity, nor assurance that the "right" moral decision will be made, the interplay among these questions and values offers a framework that will yield movement and direction. The emergent vision and direction that is born of this framework will have tended to the critical concerns that are raised by the concepts of moral character and narrative. The framework at least suggests that character ethics and an ethics of norms are indispensable to one another. It is precisely this type of pedagogy and narrative framework that ethics across the curriculum must seek to develop in our colleges and universities.

Notes

1. In this chapter I understand the idea of the ethics of character to include the ethics of virtue and the ethics of narrative as well. One of my contentions is that in contemporary usage these concepts are intertwined and that there is an integral connection between them. For an analysis of the way these ideas function in the work of Stanley Hauerwas see, Gene Outka "Character, Vision, and Narrative," *Religious Studies Review* 6 (April 1980).

2. These criticisms are articulated most explicitly in the work of Hauerwas, particularly in his *Truthfulness and Tragedy* (Notre Dame, IN: University of Notre Dame Press, 1978). They can be found however in the works of most of the writers mentioned in the text.

3. See Oliver F. Williams and John W. Houck, *Full Value* (San Francisco: Harper and Row, 1978).

4. Thomas L. Shaffer, *Faith and the Professions* (Provo, UT: Brigham Young University Press, 1987).

5. One of the most referenced articles by contemporary theorists of virtue is Edmund Pincoffs, "Quandary Ethics," *Mind* 80 (1971): 552-71.

6. These criticisms are articulated most clearly in Hauerwas's work. In particular, see "From System to Story," in *Truthfulness and Tragedy*.

7. Most contemporary treatments of the idea of character have tended to take an individualistic cast. Character and virtue have been understood to refer primarily to qualities of the self. This is an unfortunate development in ethical theory and reflects what some critics refer to as the limits of ethical theory in liberal society. The discussion on "civic virtue" that is central to some schools of social

and political theory is an important addition to the literature on virtue in ethical theory. For a discussion of how the idea of character might be developed in relationship to groups and institutions, see Donahue, "Religious Institutions as Moral Agents," in *Issues in the Labor-Management Dialogue: Church Perspectives,* ed. Adam Maida (St. Louis: Catholic Health Association of the United States, 1982).

8. Alasdair MacIntyre, *After Virtue* (Notre Dame, IN: University of Notre Dame Press, 1981), 178.

9. For the most developed treatment of the role of convictions in the moral life see the work of James McClendon, particularly his *Understanding Religious Convictions* (Notre Dame, IN: University of Notre Dame Press, 1975), and *Ethics* (Nashville: Abingdon Press, 1986).

10. The idea of vision as a moral category can be found most explicitly in the work of Iris Murdoch, particularly in *The Sovereignty of Good* (New York: Schocken Books, 1971).

11. For a fuller treatment of idea of practices, see MacIntyre's *After Virtue,* 169-89.

12. The idea of tradition is treated in greater detail in MacIntyre, *After Virtue,* 190-209.

13. A superb critical analysis of the use of casuistry in both historical and contemporary contexts can be found in Albert Jonsen and Stephen Toulmin, *The Abuse of Casuistry* (London: Oxford University Press, 1988).

14. The works of Jean Piaget, Lawrence Kohlberg, Erik Erikson, and James Fowler have been the primary sources in developmental theory that have been appropriated by writers in ethics. For an excellent summary of the offerings of these theorists for theological ethics, see James Fowler, *Becoming Adult, Becoming Christian* (San Francisco: Harper and Row, 1984).

15. This example is taken from Hauerwas, *Vision and Virtue* (Notre Dame: University of Notre Dame Press, 1974), 73-74.

16. For an insightful critique of the ethics of character see Edmund Pellegrino, "Rationality, the Normative, and Narrative in the Philosophy of Morals," in H. Tristram Engelhardt, *Knowledge, Value, and Belief* (Hastings on Hudson: The Hastings Center, 1977).

17. Thomas H. Groome, *Christian Religious Education* (San Francisco: Harper and Row, 1980).

18. Gilbert Meilaender, *The Limits of Love* (University Park: Pennsylvania State University Press, 1987).

19. For an analysis of the way that story and moral choice exist in juxtaposition, see Donahue, "Narrative Ethics and a Theology of Love," in *Bioethics Books,* vol. 1, no. 1, 1989.

20. Two examples of the individualistic use of character can be found in the work by Williams and Houck, *Full Value,* and Thomas Shaffer, *Faith and the Professions*.

21. The work of Gibson Winter, a social ethicist with a particular appreciation for the role of social science in ethics, is a much overlooked contribution to social ethics. His book *Elements for a Social Ethic* (New York: Macmillan, 1966) is a classic that would contribute valuable insights to the current discussion of character ethics.

22. Hauerwas and Yoder have on several public occasions (at meetings of the Society of Christian Ethics, the American Academy of Religion, the Washington Roundtable on Ethics) refuted the claim that their work is sectarian. For a development of the idea of a public theology, see the work of David Tracy, particularly his *Plurality and Ambiguity* (San Francisco: Harper and Row, 1987).

23. The two best attempts to develop criteria for the truthfulness of stories can be found in Terrence Tilley, *Story Theology* (Wilmington, DE: Michael Glazier, 1985), 182-214, and Michael Goldberg, *Narrative and Theology: A Critical Introduction* (Nashville: Abingdon Press, 1982).

24. For a superb summary and analysis of the major ethical issues at stake in the current theological debate on foundations, I am indebted to a paper by Douglas Ottati, "Between Foundationalism and Non-Foundationalism," presented at the Washington Ethics Roundtable, May 5, 1989.

25. See H. Richard Niebuhr, *The Meaning of Revelation* (New York: Macmillan, 1962), and *The Responsible Self: An Essay in Christian Moral Philosophy* (New York: Harper & Row, 1963). See James M. Gustafson, *Ethics from a Theocentric Perspective,* vol. 1 and 2 (Chicago: University of Chicago Press, 1984).

26. My understanding of the organic metaphor is drawn primarily from its usage in the sociology of organizations. An excellent summary of the idea can be found in Charles Perrow, *Complex Organizations* (Glenview: Scott, Foresman, and Company, 1979), 174-99.

27. The idea of a canon containing the essential truths of a tradition is developed in greater detail in David Tracy, *The Analogical Imagination* (New York: Crossroads Books, 1983).

28. The idea of conversation that I develop here derives from John Courtney Murray's famous work, *We Hold These Truths* (New York: Sheed and Ward, 1960).

29. James McClendon, *Understanding Religious Convictions* (Notre Dame, IN: University of Notre Dame Press, 1975), 7.

30. For the most thorough analysis of this concept, see Terrence Deal and Allan Kennedy, *Corporate Cultures* (Reading, MA: Addison Wesley Press, 1982).

31. Murdoch, *The Sovereignty of Good,* 53-55.

32. The most extensive and insightful work on conversion in contemporary theological ethics can be found in the work of Walter Conn. In particular, see his *Christian Conversion* (New York: Paulist Press, 1986).

33. Charles E. Curran, "The Stance of Moral Theology," in *New Perspectives in Moral Theology* (Notre Dame, IN: University of Notre Dame Press, 1974), 47-86.

34. Parts of this chapter appeard in publication previously in James A. Donahue *The Use of Virtue and Character in Applied Ethics,* Horizons 17, 2 (Fall, 1990).

Chapter 4
The Worldview Theory of Morality

In chapter 2 we presented a model of the disciplines that suggests that values exist in each one of them. This is because the fact-value distinction is not hard and fast. Within all so-called expositions of the objectivist thesis there are suppressed value statements that ought to be brought to light and examined since they affect the way the discipline does its business. This occurs in the discipline itself and its practitioners.

Because of this necessity of expressing value statements, professors in the university must find a way to create an amalgam of the objective and the subjective interacting with each other; one might very well imagine creating some sort of twin that possessed both an objective and a subjective element (Thomas Kuhn and Paul Feyerabend could be cited as philosophers who did just this—albeit in different ways).[1] Consensus and logical argument appeal to the common body of objective knowledge resident within.[2] But at the same time it is necessary to acknowledge the other aspects of *Weltanschauung*. This is especially true in moral philosophy.

Though they are subjective in nature, these worldviews are themselves subject to evaluative criteria. These criteria are formal and logical principles that are virtually devoid of empirical content. Together, these criteria can be put together to form what I call the Personal Worldview Imperative: *"All people must develop a single, comprehensive and internally coherent worldview that is good and that we strive to act out in our daily lives."*[3] It is my opinion that every agent acting or potentially acting in the world falls under the normative force of the Personal Worldview Imperative. This principle could probably be unpacked to cover a wide range of axiological issues. This is important since the question of values in the disciplines is broader than merely an examination of morality. But for our initial purposes let us examine three separate criteria that are imbedded within the Personal Worldview Imperative and which bear closer examination.

The first criterion is *We have a duty to develop and to act out our worldview*. This means that we are expected *to choose and fashion* a point of view that will do much to condition our day-to-day consciousness. It is not enough merely to accept another's general beliefs and attitudes about ethics, politics, aesthetics, and religion. If one did this, it would be tantamount to becoming the slave of another. If some modicum of freedom and autonomy are a part of our human nature, and if ultimately we are only content if we act out our human nature, then (assuming that all wish to be ultimately content), we should all seek to exercise our freedom in the most practically fundamental way by choosing and fashioning a worldview.

It may be the case that our power of choice in adopting a worldview is not absolute, but that does not prevent us from doing what we can. Let us consider the architect metaphor. A limited choice in adopting a worldview would be akin to moving into someone else's house. Suppose, upon reflection, there were many features about the house you decided you did not like (and you had some money); you might set about remodeling the house a room at a time, taking care that your remodeling scheme was according to some larger plan or aesthetic point of view. The word "fashion" is meant to embody some of this sense of "re-creation" or "remodeling."

Depending upon our circumstances, this process of fashioning a worldview could take some considerable length of time—especially given difficult exterior or interior factors beyond our control. No two people's tasks are identical.

The second criterion is *We have a duty to develop a single worldview that is both comprehensive and internally consistent.* This second duty owes its justification to rather prudential concerns of what would count as a serviceable worldview. A worldview that is not unitary and comprehensive might not give us direction at some future time when such direction is sorely needed. A worldview that is not comprehensive is not one on which we can depend to help us grow and develop in life.

Likewise, a worldview that is not internally consistent is one that might in the future offer us contradictory directions of action. This is because the areas of inconsistency (call them "A" and "non-A") might each develop a line of reasoning that maintains their original character (logical heritability). The resulting "offspring" of "A" and "non-A" would also be opposed. If these offspring are imperatives of action, then one is in a dilemma situation.[4] Such a worldview is inadequate because it may not be able to offer clear direction for action at some time in the future.

The third criterion is *We have a duty to create a worldview that is good.* This final criterion is the most difficult to justify in moral terms. Clearly, the word "good" in this instance may mean merely "good for the agent's prudential interests." Certainly, one would not want to create a worldview that was self-destructive. Who would argue that one's worldview ought to support a plan of life and development which was not personally advantageous to us?

But we would want to assert that the sort of worldview we are talking about is one that should be morally good, as well. Such a moral interpretation of the Personal Worldview Imperative is essential if this principle is to be of use in moral analysis.

The argument to give greater specification to this latter sense of "good" is what will be a guiding principle in the rest of the book. Therefore, let us begin our task.

Understanding Worldview

Worldview is an amalgam of our normative and factual views on the world. We come to life with various dictates that seize us qua organisms living in the world. These are, first, procuring food, shelter, and clothing and, second, the inclination to reproduce. These are the dictates of biology. All biological organisms "seek"[5] these primary ends.

But these ends do not make us human. They are necessary conditions for survival as organisms. We cannot become human if we are not first organisms. It seems that our brains are also structured in this way.[6] Certain essential functions (such as those that enable the physiological requirements for action) must be fulfilled in order for us to begin our journey to humanity. Once these are satisfied, we can create a reflective space by which we engage our rational faculties.

Human reason is a tool that can be used for, on the one hand, immediate practical needs as well as medium- and long-term practical needs, and on the other hand, pure (nonpragmatic) speculation. The practical needs *can* be purely self-oriented in a narrow, extrinsic fashion. This sort of direction looks to what the ego can achieve in a prudentially enhancing fashion. For example, let's say Juanita is playing marbles. We all know that the point of marbles is to hit your opponent's so that you might gain her marble. Everyone starts with the same number of marbles and the one with the most marbles at the end wins the game.

Let us also assume that Juanita is a superb marble shooter. Juanita can easily win all the marbles from the boys and girls at her playground. If we assume that the children may only buy a certain number of marbles a month out of their allowances, then Juanita is limited to playing only a few games of marbles a month (the length of time it takes her to acquire everyone else's marbles).

Juanita is utilizing what can be called a self-oriented, narrow, extrinsic reasoning. It is *self-oriented* because Juanita does not consider the feelings of the children who are losing their marbles to her superior skills. It is *narrow* because Juanita could (even on prudential grounds) gain further pleasure from gaming were she to lose once in a while in order to extend her competitive pleasures. It is *extrinsic* because Juanita is only after the victory and the consequent acquisition of other people's marbles. If she enjoyed the game for itself, then she would coach other players so that they might be able to attain her level of excellence and then she could extend her abilities beyond their current levels.

In another case, John hustles cocaine. He does this because he was born on the wrong side of the tracks. His family was entirely dysfunctional and he seeks to find the quickest way out of the bone-wrenching poverty from whence he came. John's actions are *self-oriented* because he does not consider the lives he is damaging by being a cocaine pusher. John's actions are *narrow* because he does not see that he might enhance his long-term well-being by taking a course that is legal and does not hurt others. John's actions are based upon *extrinsic* motivations. He only sees what he wants out of the transaction. He is not really interested in demonstrating and perfecting the professionalism of good salesmanship; rather, he wants his money without hassle so that he can buy the things he thinks will raise him up in the world.

In both of these cases (Juanita and John) we are dealing with egoists who are acting for what they think is their own best interest. It is my contention that in acting in just this way Juanita and John (and any others who choose this path) are fulfilling the prudential imperative of non-rational behavior. This prudential imperative has a long history. In Homer the exploits of the heroes are generally seen in terms of the prudential good.[7] However, this is not always the case. When Achilles drags Hector around Troy, Achilles thinks he is making everyone feel that he is the most *agathos* (in this context, "the greatest"). Instead, many consider it *eischron* (in this context, "a truly classless act"). Thus, even in the era when virtue was written about in terms of competitive zeal, there is still a sense of what is appropriate. Violate that sensibility—even when one displays power in its majesty—and one is judged to be bad. This "bad" is not a prudential bad, but a normative one based upon standards of propriety. These standards are put in place to check the excesses of human egoism.

The origin of the standards (attributed to the gods in the case of Homer) seek to put human excess in check. Even the greatest mental competitor of them all, Odysseus, is checked in his journey homeward by his expression of hubris.

One can see this pull of competitive versus cooperative virtues in the religions of the world as well. In Judaism, Moses is forced to submit his will to a mightier power (God) who can prohibit natural human impulses by divine command. David (the great king and conqueror), also, is humbled by his sin of lusting after another man's wife. This sin involved the murder of her husband and profiting by this murder. But David is shown that he cannot act as he pleases with impunity.[8]

In Hinduism, the dialogues between Lord Krishna and Arjuna in the *Bhagavad Gita* suggest the role of self-control in the elevation of the soul above the natural inclinations of Maya.[9]

Siddhartha also explored how one might steer a middle path between personal excess and the will to power and a middle path that is found through the extinction of desire.[10]

Plato provides us with two classic cases of this conflict through the characters of Thrasymachus and Callicles as they confront their Socrates. Plato's Socrates faces their bald krateristic egoism with the tenets (a) justice is *not* the rule of the strongest; and (b) it is better to suffer injustice than to do it.[11] This is a radical move away from the purely competitive, egoistic standard. The justification turns out to be a quasi-religious (I would say Hindu-influenced) understanding of psychic harmony and personal flourishing.

Aristotle also moves in the direction away from purely egoistic *self-interested, narrow,* and *extrinsic* motivation to one that incorporates both balance and an appreciation of the other person (in the case of pleasure and true friendships).[12] A person develops virtues of character because only these will cause contentment of his soul and allow him to flourish as a person (*eudaimonia*).

In each of these cases there is a contrast made between the competitive, egoistic model outlined earlier and *something else.* This something else varies but at the very least it contains provisions for a person being honored for actions that were not all about winning wars at all costs, asserting of the individual will at all costs, gaining power at all costs, becoming "successful" in the eyes of the world at all costs. The proviso "at all costs" means that the end in question is so valuable that one may do anything he can get away with to obtain it. Thus, if Richard III or Macbeth wants to ascend to the throne, he can murder a relative or a mentor in the process. The prize sits for the taking. All comers are invited to grasp for it come what may, no holds barred—whatever!

This sort of position can be termed 'kraterism', after the Greek term for power. It is an approach to the world that says that we are free to do anything we want to get what we want. A kraterist is not perfectly free to do anything he wants. This is because there are other agents who also aspire after the prize. These other aspirants will get in his way to try to stop him. Thus, his freedom of action is limited by his competitors.

The kraterist is also limited by the institutions of the society in which he lives. These limitations are only as strong as their enforcement provisions. For example, if I lived in country A that had a law against the cultivation, processing, and sale of cocaine and strictly enforced its laws by active policing and a free and protected legal system, then I, as a kraterist, would be severely limited in my ability to become a cocaine kingpin.

However, if I, as a kraterist, were to live in country B that had a law against the cultivation, processing, and sale of cocaine but the law was never enforced either through strict policing or through a protected legal system, then I would be much more free to practice my occupation of cocaine businessman.

It is one thing to restrict my activities via external constraint and the threat of punishment and another to restrict my activities via internal sanctions against engaging in certain sorts of activities. In the former case I do not exert my kraterism, merely because of various prudential calculations. It's not because I've suddenly become a good man. It's merely that I calculate that my chance for success versus my chance of being caught weigh against my acting as I please. In the words of a former teacher of mine (Richard Posner), criminals will cease to be criminals when crime doesn't pay.

But what if a person had a "reasonable-to-good chance" of getting away with it, but still did not assert his kraterism? Obviously, this would not be a kraterist. The egoist-cum-kraterist will never check his grab for power and all that goes with it. This is the nature of the beast.

But other nonkraterists *will* check their prudential gains. They do so because they allow other principles to trump their prudential interests. These other interests generally represent other values. When these other values concern other agents, as such, we call these considerations moral. The "moral turn," therefore, concerns that point at which another value trumps the egoist-cum-krateristic imperative so that a person turns away from a course of action that is prudentially advantageous. From the krateristic perspective this is irrational. From the moral perspective this is required—a duty.

We have now entered the realm of morality.

In the realm of morality a person does not assert prudential kraterism at all costs. Because of one's perceived ethical duty she forgoes pursuing certain prudential interests. But why? The reasons are varied and represent the foundations of the major moral theories. I have always highlighted intuitionism, virtue ethics, utilitarianism, and deontology as the principal moral theories. There are, of course, others.[13] However, the point here is not to be exhaustive but to be illustrative concerning the question at hand: why forgo prudential advantage for some moral duty? The Intuitionists will say that we immediately grasp this to be true either on the level of principle or on the level of action.[14] The advocate of virtue ethics would cite the formation of character and its attendant virtues (one of which is self-control) as justification for sometimes acting contrary to our self-interest. The utilitarian will point to general utility. Sometimes pursuing my own interests will go against the good of the whole. In these instances I must refrain from pursuing my personal interests. Finally, the deontologist will set forth commands grounded in duties that are themselves (generally) rooted in logic itself. Because we are rational animals, and because we repudiate our very humanity by acting contrary to a command of reason, we must sometimes not pursue prudential ends.

Each of these reasons not to pursue prudential ends constitutes its own moral theory. Normative ethics concerns itself with these theories and how they answer this fundamental question of morality.

One pole in the criteria of choosing a theory is its logical structure and the other is its resonance with an individual's worldview. The logical evaluation of moral theories is more the purview of advanced philosophical analysis. Thus it is less useful to use in the university as a whole. Thus we are left with an examination of personal worldview. But how does one get in touch with his worldview? We all live with worldviews or else we could not effectively act. But what exactly is a worldview? How do we come to know it? How do we live with it?

A worldview contains two sorts of propositions: those that represent statements of fact and those that represent statements of value.[15] These do not neatly segregate (as argued earlier) so that all of one sort are on the right side and all of the other are on the left. No. There is much overlap. Most every statement of fact has value-laden dimensions that can become apparent upon careful inspection. Most statements of value depend upon certain factual understandings about the world and the rules that govern it. This having been said, it is important when one conducts an inventory of one's beliefs and knowledge claims that she acknowledge these types of understandings so that she might properly test each in its own domain.

There are two ways to examine a worldview: from the macro perspective and from the micro perspective. I liken this to the phenotype-genotype distinction made in biology. It is the macro perspective that presents to us the person that lives in the world. This is an entity that is presented in whole.

It is the micro perspective that is largely (though not entirely) responsible for the macro perspective. At the micro perspective we have each of the major value categories: ethics, religion, and aesthetics. There are also various dispositions to believe certain facts about the world. These are crucial, too, because they account for an agent's understanding of the underlying mechanisms of the natural world.

Just as the phenotype is not completely reducible to the genotype,[16] so also is it the case that the macro perspective of the agent is not completely reducible to the particular values and facts that she espouses.

How Worldview Analysis Can Advance
Ethics across the Curriculum

If we were to summarize the personal worldview imperative it would enjoin us to:

- *Create a consistent worldview*
- *Create a complete worldview*
- *Create a good worldview*
- *Put our worldview into action*

What might this mean in the context of various courses within the university? First, let us look at consistency. Many disciplines already endorse consistency in their approach to teaching. For example, English teachers grade students down for creating inconsistent body paragraphs in their essays. Biochemists are upset when one is performing an experiment and in his lab technique he titrates one solution after one fashion and the next after a different fashion. Because of the principle of consistency, it is held that if the student does not treat all his samples in the same manner, his results are false.

Likewise in the business school, a student would be taught that a company must adopt a mission statement and adhere to it in a consistent manner. Without such a disposition, corporate identification (an essential feature for successful marketing) is impossible.

In all three cases (English, biochemistry, and business management) it is the case that consistency is considered to be a characteristic of all good practitioners of the discipline. This sense of good is prudential (non-moral). It merely reflects the functional ability to perform most (or all) of the requisite criteria. Since this much is *already* agreed upon, it is not too great a stretch to think about extending the *range* of application. In this case we would take consistency one step further to include the worldview of the student. Let's revisit the examples.

In the first case the English student is exhorted not only to be consistent in the argument he presents in his paper, but also to be consistent in the argument presented and his own personal value system. For example, if a person were appalled by male sexism that translated into the subjugation of women, he might integrate his personal convictions in an essay evaluating a novel by Ernest Hemingway or Norman Mailer.

The English teacher who "buys into" this pedagogy will encourage her students to bring in their own opinions in a reasoned manner so that they might experience personal consistency between their private consciousness and their personae as students in the university.

Likewise the biochemistry teacher might not only exhort consistent lab technique, but also engage her students in issues of value consistency were they to become professional researchers. In this case, one could imagine talk of what a researcher who believed that a fertilized egg was human might do were she to be engaged in genetic research (that depends at least indirectly on the use of fertilized eggs that have been arrested from their normal development). Should the scientist merely be a robot performing experiments according to the approved protocol? What about the scientist's personal values and the consistency between what she is as a nonscientist person and what she is being asked to do as a scientist?

Finally, in the same fashion the management student should be encouraged to think about the consistency between his private values and what his job is asking him to do. When you see your company is hiding losses to artificially prop up share value, should you come forward and make a statement? Can you afford *NOT* to if consistency is indeed a moral criterion?

In each case it is our contention that taking consistency from its already comfortable level of professional excellence to the next level of human integration into the social role of that job transforms consistency discussions from the prudential to the moral. If we are going to prepare our students to be morally aware agents living in the world, we must make the jump from functional consistency to moral consistency.

The same sort of argument may be made concerning completeness. In a strange way completeness is rather hard to understand. We all intuit that to be complete means that the theory can handle novel cases. But this is not the end of the story. There is much more. Completeness requires that we understand the boundaries of our discipline. No theory can be complete unless we understand what is *not* covered by the theory. This is often a difficult exercise. This is because most academics believe that their discipline is the be-all and end-all of everything worthy to be known. But if that were really true, then the conjecture about that discipline's completeness would be unproven.

Instead (ironically), completeness should not envision the infinite but rather the finite. We must come to a realization of what *is not* within the discipline. This sensibility of limitation is also a powerful ingredient in worldview analysis. At the writing of this book (2000-2002), the dot-com industry experienced a depression after an exhilarating rise. Many dot-com CEOs actually believed that they (and their companies—an extension of themselves) were unlimited. All the old rules of economics concerning finance were passé. Price-earnings ratios need not be burdened with the 5 to 1 or 10 to 1 rules; instead PEs could be 500 to 1 with no trouble because growth would make up the old "risk corridor."

The instructor of economics should think about completeness in this context not only to support traditional theories of risk assessment (functional completeness), but also to think about more human-metaphysical concepts such as "why should the rules suddenly change and what is the consequence of such changes upon the lives of real people living in the world?" Completeness in this second sense (the ethical sense) entails consideration of where the boundaries of economics should be and what are the (ethical) consequences of changing them. In this way completeness is an essential part of the economics curriculum both in its functional and in its moral sense.

Next, we should consider whether the course of action considered is good. Part of the reason that this question is rarely asked is because most academics consider the question of goodness to be overly subjective. This is because it is most often the case that most disciplines rarely explore any sense of good save functional, prudential goodness. These teachers feel that if students want to delve further into questions of moral goodness they need only take a class in philosophy or theology. Since the writers of this volume are a philosopher and a theologian we are loath to turn back students from our classes; however, this should not shackle teachers in other disciples from approaching issues of goodness of professional practice. Surely, every historian has a notion of what counts as plagiarism. Plagiarism is not good professional practice. It is also not good moral conduct because it is an instance of stealing. Thus, it is entirely appropriate for a historian to decry popular historians who may have been accused of plagiarism for both functional and moral reasons.

We have found in our faculty ethics workshop that many professors are timid about discussing issues of goodness, as such. This is because they feel ill prepared to confront the wide variety of student questions on this topic. The only solutions to this are 1) a firm statement by the administration that they encourage such discourse in the classroom and that "incidents" of the same will not be "held against" the professor, and 2) a clear policy of faculty development in which workshops and grants are available in order to aid professors so that they might feel more confident in addressing these topics.

The question of goodness can be suppressed by professors who are unwilling to discuss it. However, when this happens the entire university is diminished.

Finally is the question of acting out one's convictions of goodness in her daily life. This is one of the most difficult questions of all. In post-9/11 America we all stood in awe when volunteers from Connecticut, New York, and New Jersey descended upon the scene of what once was the World Trade Center to offer assistance to those in need. The support personnel were extraordinary! There were doctors, nurses, retired military, police, firefighters, and off-duty personnel and concerned citizens of all sorts who pitched in to help.

Likewise, there were the passengers on the flight that was crashed in Pennsylvania who apparently overcame the terrorists to thwart their plan of extensive death and destruction.

Acting out one's beliefs is critical to creating morally conscious individuals. Whether we are talking about an art historian who decides that a painting is a fake (and might lose his job as the result of his decision) or the athletic coach who must suspend a star athlete (for conduct violations) even though it will mean the team will lose the title, the principle of standing up for one's beliefs and not being a hypocrite is an essential lesson for all disciplines to express.

Conclusion

The reason that the worldview approach to values theory is so compelling is that it embraces people as they are: composites of fact and value together striving to act in the world. What one must try to avoid in presenting the worldview theory of morality and values is a move toward relativism. There are firm criteria found within the Personal Worldview Imperative meant to exclude relativism. It is important to make this clear to professors who choose this model to implement ethics across the curriculum at their university.

However, the flexibility of the worldview approach can capture students in a way that other approaches cannot. This is because of its centering its attention at the individuals situated in the realm of action. This is the arena in which they live. What we suggest is that these criteria of consistency, completeness, goodness, and implementation can move students beyond the functional requirements set by their disciplines to a higher standard of consideration of these terms in an ethical context. This is, therefore, the arena in which interdisciplinary integration is possible. It is the basis by which ethics across the curriculum can evolve from traditional treatments of subject matter to an extended sense of what it means to be a student at the university.

Notes

1. Thomas S. Kuhn, *The Structure of Scientific Revolutions,* 2nd ed. (Chicago: University of Chicago Press, 1970), and Paul Feyerabend, *Against Method* (London: Verso, 1975) and *Realism, Rationalism, and Scientific Method* (Cambridge: Cambridge University Press, 1981), have prominently called into question the dispassionate objectivity in science. Their work owes a debt to Willard Quine, who wrestled with finding ways to try and express a give-and-take developmental process in which the individual and the world interact with each other. In the end Quine's amalgam seeks to emphasize the objective. See "Natural Kinds" in *Ontological Relativity and Other Essays* (New York: Columbia University Press, 1969). Kuhn and Feyerabend, on the other hand, set out an analysis which emphasizes more strongly the force of the subjective.

2. "The common body of knowledge" is meant to refer to objective-leaning statements that are accepted as true (such as Newton's three laws of motion) along with statements of commonly held core values (such as the virtues of courage, self-control, justice, and wisdom).

3. Some might contend that my depiction of this imperative places an overreliance upon form over content. It is a "procedure" and thus cannot have normative "content." Against this attack, it can be said that though the prescription *simpliciter* is procedural, it will result in some content. And, if taken in the Socratic spirit of living an examined life, then the force of the normativity is toward participation in a process which must be sincere because it represents each of our very best versions of the "good, true, and beautiful."

4. A moral dilemma occurs when one, through no fault of his or her own, finds him- or herself in the situation that the only available choices of action are both evil.

5. To "seek" in this instance invokes teleological language but it is essentially metaphorical. For a discussion of teleological explanations as metaphor see Larry Wright, *Teleological Explanations* (Berkeley: University of California Press, 1976).

6. For a fine discussion of the development and functions of the brain see Louise H. Marshall and Horace W. Mangoun eds., *Discoveries in the Human Brain: Neuroscience Prehistory, Brain Structures, and Function* (Totowa, NY: Humana Press, 1998).

7. Writers who have documented the nuances of this process are E.R. Dodds, *The Greeks and the Irrational* (Berkeley: University of California Press, 1951), and A. W. H. Adkins in a classic rendition of the struggle between the competitive and the cooperative virtues as described in *Merit and Responsibility* (Oxford: Blackwells, 1959, reprinted Chicago: Midway, 1974).

8. 2 *Samuel,* chapter 11.

9. *Bhagavad Gita,* ed., trans. W. G. P. Hill (London: Oxford University Press, 1928).

10. *Samyutta,* ed. Leon Feer (London: Pali Text Society, 1960), vol. 420-23.

11. These arguments are made by Plato in *Republic,* book I, through five distinct arguments, and in the *Gorgias.*

12. It is true that utility friendships are not much better than the egoistic models above except that they are modified by the person who has cultivated the proper virtues of character. See Aristotle's discussion in *Nicomachean Ethics* 8.3-6.

13. The most important moral theories that Boylan has excluded are the noncognitivist theories, such as Emotivism; however, the points above are generally applicable to these as well.

14. I call these level-one and level-two intuitionism, respectively. For a discussion of these see Boylan, *Basic Ethics* (Upper Saddle River, NJ: Prentice Hall, 2000), chapter 1.

15. I am in accord here with Quine's insistence that analytic and synthetic truths do not easily segregate. See "Two Dogmas of Empiricism," in *From a Logical Point of View* (Cambridge, MA: Harvard University Press, 1953).

16. See Alan Garfinkel, *Forms of Explanation* (New Haven, CT: Yale University Press, 1981), 49-74; J. Sterelny and Philip Kitcher, "The Return of the Gene," *Journal of Philosophy* 85:7 (July 1988): 339-61. The point of these essays is to assert that the reductionist notion of complete bottom-up causation is flawed. There is, rather, a more complicated interaction between the lower and upper levels.

Chapter 5
The Embedded-Values Approach

To be human is to be engaged in a moral enterprise. Our approach to ethics across the curriculum is based on the assumption that there are implicit ethical responsibilities and obligations in all human actions and that the role of university education is to create understanding about the nature and form of our moral engagements, particularly as they relate to the information and knowledge that is imparted in the formal curriculum. Universities must provide a framework and occasions for uncovering the tacit and implicit ethical dimensions of the moral lives of students. The idea of embedded values is critical to developing this moral consciousness.

Embeddedness: An Introduction

"What would you like for your birthday? A new vacuum cleaner or world peace?" Sounds like a ridiculous question, doesn't it? But what makes it ridiculous? It is the disparity in the fundamental quality of the goods involved. On the one hand, you have a vacuum cleaner whose task is to remove the dirt in your rug or on your floor. If vacuum cleaners didn't exist, we would beat our carpets outside and sweep our floors. If we didn't beat and sweep, we'd sneeze a bit more, but we would still live. All of our primary goods of agency—on the *first level* food, clothing, and shelter that allow us to live and actually *be agents,* and on the *second level* those goods necessary to *be effective agents* (such as education and the recognition of fundamental human dignity)—are unaffected by the existence or nonexistence of a vacuum cleaner.

However, if one lived in a land that was torn by war, these two levels of primary goods would be in jeopardy. It is very probable that the second level would be interrupted. When war occurs, the normal operations of the society are discontinued. These include the schooling and social service structure that are so necessary in providing this supportive environment. When war occurs, the society is often cut back to a survivalist mode.

In the survivalist mode there may or may not be enough to eat. The twentieth century is certainly full of examples of cities in the midst of war that have had to resort to extreme measures in order to survive.[1] Thus, in war it is possible that every agent may be at risk concerning his or her basic goods of agency at the first as well as the second level.

Beyond the basic goods of agency there are other goods that we either possess or seek to possess. I call these goods "secondary goods." These include property (both real and portable) and intangible goods such as social status and self-esteem. The secondary goods are divided according to their relationship to the basic conditions of action: 1) life-enhancing, 2) useful, and 3) luxurious. These other goods are proximately or remotely related to effective action.[2] I contend that moral claim for goods decreases as one moves away from the basic conditions of action. Thus, for example, being a member of a social class that faces discrimination within a society is far closer to effective action (life-enhancing) than possessing a portable compact disc music player (luxurious). This means that the good involved (respecting the member of the discriminated class) has greater moral value than possessing the portable compact disc music player.[3] This is because being discriminated against (like African Americans in the United States) can negatively affect one's self-esteem and ability to be an effective agent. Since it is assumed that, before anything else, each of us wants to commit voluntary, purposive action; anything that is an unfair[4] hindrance to this strikes against our fundamental nature as humans. Each person alive on the earth—now or at any time, anywhere—can legitimately claim to fulfill what is his natural potential (at least respecting fundamental human agency). If there is a reciprocal relation between legitimate claims to goods by individuals (and groups of individuals) and the duty of the society to provide those goods to said individuals, then this distinction about proximity to action is very important.

This is because the society has a *duty* to provide said individuals with those goods that are proximate to action—either as basic goods or as secondary goods that are very fundamental/life-enhancing (such as not being discriminated against). However, society *does not* have a duty to provide agents with goods that might be useful for action, but are not fundamental. For example, it might be useful to own a cell phone. One might be a more effective agent with a cell phone, but it still does not pass the test for being a fundamental secondary good since one can still fulfill a large range of effective action without one. A cell phone is nice, but it is not necessary.[5] A cell phone is not fundamentally life-enhancing and is several levels removed from basic goods.

Thus, targeting society's resources toward alleviating the negative consequences of discrimination would be (on this account) more morally defensible than using society's resources to provide people cell phones. And on our earlier example, since the basic goods of agency are of far greater importance (to human agency[6]) than secondary goods, it is clear that one would choose world peace over a new vacuum cleaner.

The general point here is that (concerning moral issues), there is a hierarchy of claims to goods that may be ranked according to their proximity to action. In the first class there are *basic goods*. These are ranked on two levels. These levels correspond to their proximity to one's ability to act (the most primary, natural purpose of every human agent). On the *first level* are those goods that are biologically related to acting at all: food (a minimum number of calories given a certain body mass), clothing (protection of the core body temperature so that it might be above 94 degrees Fahrenheit), and shelter (providing core body temperature protection and reasonable safety for sleeping). On the *second level* are those goods necessary to act effectively within a historical/geographical society. (In the United States in the twenty-first century, it would include: literacy, basic mathematical skills, basic computer skills, and some familiarity with the culture that has shaped our civilization.)

After basic goods are *secondary goods*. These include the life-enhancing goods (concerned with making life more bearable relative to other agents in the society), the useful goods (concerned practically with enhancing action at levels more concerned with efficiency than equity), and the luxurious goods (those goods that convey pleasure but are not essential for action).[7]

Since basic goods are more essential for action than secondary goods, moral rights claims for basic goods will trump secondary goods rights claims. Within each category, the level more primary to action will take precedence over the less primary.

All of these rights claims are grounded in the definition of what it means to be an agent and an objective evaluation of what every agent deems primary to him or her above all else (i.e., the ability to execute purposive action).

Thus, on the moral level the term "embeddedness" refers to the proximity to the conditions of action (as discussed above). Underlying this is the notion that what is natural for all agents to desire most (the ability to commit free, purposive action) is also justified. This can be set out more exactly in the following argument.

The Argument for the Moral Status of Basic Goods

1. Before anything else, all people desire to act—Fact
2. Whatever all people desire before anything else is natural to that species—Fact
3. Desiring to act is natural to *Homo sapiens*—1, 2
4. People value what is natural to them—Assertion
5. What people value, they wish to protect—Assertion
6. All people wish to protect their ability to act, beyond all else—1, 3, 4, 5
7. The strongest interpersonal "oughts" are expressed via our highest value systems: religion, morality, and aesthetics—Assertion
8. All people must agree, upon pain of logical contradiction, that what is natural and desirable to them individually is natural and desirable to everyone collectively and individually—Assertion
9. Everyone must seek personal protection for her own ability to act via religion, morality, and/or aesthetics—6, 7
10. Everyone, upon pain of logical contradiction, must admit that all other humans will seek personal protection of their ability to act via religion, morality, and/or aesthetics—8, 9
11. All people must agree, upon pain of logical contradiction, that since the attribution of the basic goods of agency are predicated generally, that it is inconsistent to assert idiosyncratic preferences—Fact
12. Goods that are claimed through generic predication apply equally to each agent and everyone has a stake in their protection—10, 11

13. Justified rights claims (to goods) and duties (to provide goods) are correlative—Assertion
14. Everyone has at least a moral right to the basic goods of agency and others in the society have a duty to provide those goods to all—12, 13

If this argument is correct, then morality is all about allowing people to pursue the goods of action within some context. Those goods most proximate garner the highest degree of respect (and accompanying duties against the society) while those goods more remote garner less.

The Concept of Relative Embeddedness

The first section of this chapter sketched out the notion of moral embeddedness. In this section we will explore the dynamics of various imperatives for action. These may include imperatives of value (such as ethics, religion, and aesthetics). For the purposes of this chapter the imperatives of value will be limited to ethics and prudence.

The prudential realm is that area which promotes self-advantage. Without an intervening set of circumstances to the contrary, we will always choose that which brings us the most advantage. This seems commonplace. When we enter a restaurant and look at the menu we do *not* say, "I like eggplant lasagna, but I'll take the veal instead because it sickens me." No. We order the entrée that is most appealing to us.

Likewise with other decisions. We choose what we calculate (on some level or other) will bring us the most pleasure. This is, of course, complicated by calculations of the long and short term as well as other possible side effects. But in the main, prudential cost-benefit analysis is the principal decision-making model.

A third imperative comes from one's profession. This may be related to the prudential model, but is somewhat different. In the prudential model one is only concerned with herself. Personal pleasure (or calculations about personal pleasure) rule.[8] Professionalism moves one away from purely personal considerations to those of the group. One enters a profession of like-minded individuals to learn the practices of the profession and to partially submerge the self to a greater purpose. This purpose is largely determined by the history of the profession.

Obviously, there are potential problems when the profession itself is corrupt—such as the Mafia. One may in this case submit to a brotherhood of thieves and murderers. Effacing the self to a profession that is corrupt is not ethical. Presumably this judgment must be made at the start with rather imperfect knowledge. No one knows for sure what a profession is like from the outside. Some professions (such as the law) have initiates who come to its bar with various misconceptions. These misconceptions may either overly glorify or vilify the profession based upon extreme cases.

However, given that we are responsible for what we do, each person must make up her own mind on this matter before entering the profession (even if the information available might not be the best).

Professions create their own dictates. These imperatives spring from the internal structure of the profession. The worldview of a profession sets a standard of what it means to be a good lawyer, doctor, electrician, and so forth.[9] Thus, it is possible to have an imperative from the profession that might be contrary to another imperative (from morality or from prudence).

Example 1: A Conflict between Professional and
Prudential Imperatives

Case: Rufus has come into your clinic with severe lacerations. His partner discloses to you that Rufus has AIDS. You are a physician. Because of the severe bleeding, you are personally at risk of infection. Rufus is not in a stable condition. You cannot ship him elsewhere in his condition or he will die. You can choose to stabilize Rufus in your clinic (and risk personal infection) or ship him to the nearest hospital.

Medical imperatives: 1) It is held that physicians and healthcare professionals must put the interests of their patients first even if this means exposing themselves to personal harm.[10] 2) The Hippocratic oath says a physician will do no harm to his or her patient.

Prudential imperative: No one wants to die.

Conflicting imperatives: 1) The professional imperative says that you should treat Rufus. 2) The personal prudential imperative says that you should ship Rufus to the nearest hospital even if it means his certain death.

The above example illustrates that conflicts can occur between professional and prudential concerns. In this case one is pitting life against life. Both imperatives are very fundamental to their decision-making structure. Thus we can describe them both as deeply embedded.

A second example pits morality, professional practice, and prudential interests against each other.

Example 2: Imperative of Morality, Professional Practice, and Prudential Interests

Case: You are a German SS agent whose job it is to find Jews who are in hiding and arrest them for extermination in the concentration camps. You discover a young girl in hiding who resembles your own daughter. You are also a devout Catholic who believes in the sanctity of human life. You might be able to bring her to your house and pass her off as a relative. However, the penalty for breaking the rules is death. You have seen other officers who have had their brains blown out by superiors who were upset at their rule breaking. You value your own life.

Professional imperative: This imperative says to ferret out all Jews and send them to their death.

Moral imperative: To uphold all the basic rights of personal agency—the most fundamental being life itself. This would demand that you bring the girl into your household and pass her off as a relative.

Prudential imperative: Being killed for your actions is too high a price to pay. Turn the girl over to her almost certain death.

Conflicting imperatives: Obviously, the professional and prudential imperatives dictate turning the girl over to her almost certain death. The moral imperative stands against these. All three are fundamental to their definitions and are thus deeply embedded.

It is my contention that whenever equally embedded imperatives conflict, that the moral imperative will trump prudential and professional imperatives.[11] My argument for morality being of greater weight than prudential and professional imperatives hearkens back to the end of the last section. The purpose of that argument was to support the *moral status of basic goods*. It is important here to be clear about how we are using language. I view morality (ethics[12]) as the science of the right and wrong in human action. Along with religion and aesthetics, the terms of

commendation in ethics trump all prudential and professional imperatives. Thus, if my argument in the first section of this chapter is correct,
then there is an ethical duty to protect the basic goods of all people.
Thus, when imperatives of ethics are equally embedded with those of
prudence and professional practice, I believe it to be clear (from my prior
argument) that the imperatives of ethics should (all other things being
equal) dictate action. However there are other cases in which these various levels conflict with *different* levels of embeddedness. In these cases
prudence may be more deeply embedded than ethics. For purposes of
simplicity let us categorize the levels of embeddedness as surface, medium, and deep. We can depict them via a chart as follows.

Let us use this example: the case of the SS agent.

Demonstrating the Levels of Embeddedness

IMPERATIVE/Level of Embeddedness:	SURFACE	MEDIUM	DEEP
Professional duty: Turn over the girl			X
Prudential duty: Turn over the girl			X
Ethical duty: Do not turn over the girl			X

In this example, all the situations were deeply embedded. When all
levels of analysis indicate equal levels of embeddedness, the moral imperative rules. Let us consider a third example.

*Example 3: Unequal Moral-Prudential
Embeddedness—The Group vs. the Individual*

Case: The state of Maryland has determined that it is in the best interests
of the state to accept the recommendations of its blue-ribbon commission
of advisors and build the so-called outer beltway around Washington in
such a way that it also efficiently connects traffic to Baltimore. As a result, the law has called on them to condemn all the properties within this
building area and take possession of them under the legal power of eminent domain. Mr. and Mrs. John Q. Public live in a comfortable rambler

house on property that has been in the family for two generations. John and his wife Judy are very opposed to the outer beltway. They feel that their right to their secondary good of property is more important than any old highway. They challenge the state's right of foreclosure in court.

Prudential imperative (from the state's point of view): The practical happiness of the region in general would be greatly enhanced if this region (between Baltimore, Washington's outer suburbs, and the I-95 corridor) were connected. It would produce jobs and increased economic prosperity for the citizens. The road must go through.

Prudential imperative (from the family's point of view): It is inconvenient to move. There are no children (who might have to change schools), but there are established routines that will be interrupted.

Moral imperative (from the family's point of view): The state is using its force to deny the family of its family home, the one in which John Q. Public grew up. Though the family is financially compensated according to the findings of three independent real estate adjusters for the value of their property, this constitutes a loss of control of real estate. Real estate is a level-two secondary moral good.

Moral imperative (from the state's point of view): There is no moral imperative. This is purely a prudential decision.

IMPERATIVE/Level of Embeddedness:

	SURFACE	MEDIUM	DEEP
Prudential duty of the state:			
Build the road			X
Prudential duty of the family:			
Fight the road			X
Moral good of the family:			
Secondary useful good		X	

In this case the prudential duties of the family and of the state are of equal status. They are both deeply embedded. If one were to consider nothing else, then the state would win. This is because in cases of prudence only, the state's interests dictate action. The argument for this rests upon standard utilitarian arguments.[13] In cases only involving pleasures, more is greater than less. When a democratically elected state creates a law, it is assumed that the process insures a result according to this paradigm.[14]

When we bring ethics into the picture, the issue of embeddedness is brought to the fore. A secondary good that is at the level of useful is one level removed from the essentials of action. This can be shown through the accompanying table.

TABLE 1: The Table of Embeddedness

Basic Goods
Level-One: *Most Deeply Embedded*[15] (that which is absolutely necessary for human action)
- Food
- Clothing
- Shelter
- Protection from unwarranted bodily harm

Level-Two: *Deeply Embedded* (that which is necessary for effective basic action within a given society)
- Literacy in the language of the country in which one lives
- Basic mathematical skills
- Other fundamental skills necessary to be an effective agent in that country; e.g., in the United States some computer literacy is necessary
- Some familiarity with the culture and history of that country
- The assurance that those you interact with are not lying to promote their own interests
- The assurance that those you interact with will recognize your human dignity (as per above) and not exploit you as a means only
- Basic human rights such as those listed in the U.S. Bill of Rights and the United Nations Universal Declaration of Human Rights

Secondary Goods
Life-enhancing: *Medium to High-Medium Embeddedness*
- Basic societal respect
- Equal opportunity to compete for the prudential goods of society

- Ability to pursue a life plan according to the Personal Worldview Imperative
- Ability to participate equally as an agent in the Shared Community Worldview Imperative

Useful: *Medium to Low-Medium Embeddedness*
- Ability to utilize one's real and portable property in the manner she chooses
- Ability to gain from and exploit the consequences of one's labor regardless of starting point
- Ability to pursue goods that are generally owned by most citizens; e.g., in the United States today a telephone, television, and automobile would fit into this class

Luxurious: *Low Embeddedness*
- Ability to pursue goods that are pleasant even though they are far removed from action and from the expectations of most citizens within a given country; e.g., in the United States today a European vacation would fit into this class
- Ability to exert one's will so that she might extract a disproportionate share of society's resources for her own use

What is the justification for this classification? Let us start at the beginning. I have parsed the basic goods into two levels. The first level is the most deeply embedded. On this level there is an appeal to the *biological* conditions of agency. What does every human need in order to act, from a biological point of view? Every person needs so many calories (based on a number of different variables such as body mass and metabolic rate) on a regular basis. Without this requisite number of calories the individual will not be able to act, but instead will become sick and eventually die. The same is true with the categories of clothing and shelter. These are for the sake of maintaining a core body temperature and protecting the individual from the ravages of nature. In more temperate climates, there is less of a need for clothing, but generally some need, nonetheless, for shelter (to protect the individual from storms and high winds). Finally is the related item of protection from unwarranted bodily harm. If a person lived in the forest without any shelter, there are many predators (large and small) that might attack him. One cannot—from a biological point of view—live this way for long. When we sleep we are vulnerable to attacks of all sorts. If we are totally unprotected, it is probable we will suffer.

The above considerations are important. But there are many other necessary biological requirements. These may have to do with health and the proper operation of our bodies, etc. I have not set these out because my purpose here has been to highlight those goods that might be able to be provided by society.[16]

The second level of basic goods (deeply embedded) concentrates upon providing the agent with the goods necessary to be an effective actor within a particular society. These goods are what any agent could claim in order to act at a basic level of proficiency within that society. These goods are of two types. The first sort of second-level basic good refers to education and skills that are necessary within some society. Because these requirements are societally/historically specific, there is some relativism regarding the actual goods involved. However, regarding the more theoretical requirement, viz., that there are goods affecting education and skills that all members of that society need in order to be effective agents at a basic level, there is no relativity.

The second sort of level-two basic goods are those having to do with human liberties such as those set out in the U.S. Bill of Rights and the United Nations Universal Declaration of Human Rights. These goods are also necessary in order to be effective actors in any given society.

The secondary goods have three levels. In the first level are the life-enhancing goods (medium to high-medium embeddedness). These goods seek to enable the agent to be able to compete at an equal starting line. These goods are not as important as basic goods because basic goods enable a) the biological conditions of action and b) the basic societal skills as well as the basic human rights that allow any effective action. However, that is not to say that life-enhancing secondary goods are in any way trivial. They are not. They promote equality of action and equal opportunity.

The next level of secondary goods are those that are useful to us (medium to low-medium embeddedness). These goods are the prudential goods that most of us strive for as a primary precondition to living the sort of life that will make us happy. Again, there is some relativity here because what might make one person pleased in one country/historical era might not satisfy another.

The lowest level of secondary goods are the luxury goods (low embeddedness). These goods are aimed at providing pleasurable accessories to action. Luxury goods come in all sorts of packages. Some are small (such as gourmet coffee beans) while others are very large (such as a membership in an exclusive country club). The point here is that this class is the farthest removed from the fundamental conditions for action. If we agree with the assessment of table 1, then the embeddedness of the family's claim to useful good is less primary than the practical claims of the state. In this case the family's prudential embeddedness equals the state's prudential embeddedness. But in cases of prudential claims only, utilitarianism rules the day. Thus on prudential grounds alone, the state's claims are stronger.

The family's moral claim is at a medium level of embeddedness (because of the nature of the good at stake) and this is lower than the state's prudential claims. Thus the family's moral claim does not overturn the state's prudential claim. The new road project may proceed.

Some might claim that this case is really closet utilitarianism all the way (not simply confined to the prudential realm). Such a detractor might say that I am not really comparing deontological duties that exist on different levels of embeddedness, but rather merely justifying an action on the basis of aggregate or average utility.

I would respond to this charge by asserting that the basis of my assigning levels of goods is the proximity of that good to action. At the basic level, this is a fairly objective standard. There may be some dispute about how I have arranged goods at the secondary level. (This dispute would revolve around the classification of life-enhancing and useful goods. I also assume that there may be some controversy about what might be counted as a luxurious good.) However, I believe that the demarcation between basic and secondary is fully defensible and reasonably uncontroversial. This distinction has nothing to do with aggregate happiness but solely with the proximity of said good to action, *simpliciter*.

A fourth example can further illustrate moral embeddedness.

Example 4: Unequal Moral-Prudential
Embeddedness—Individual vs. Individual

Case: Your grandmother is dying. Your grandmother is in great psychic and moderate physical distress. Your grandmother has always had an intense fear of death and disease and has never handled bad news well. The physician tells you that if your grandmother can maintain a positive attitude she can live another year relatively pain free. If she becomes overly agitated, her condition will worsen, her physical pain will increase greatly, and her death will be much sooner. You are sitting with your grandmother and she asks you whether she will be all right (meaning that she won't die but will get better).

Prudential imperative: You don't want your grandmother to have a premature and hastened death. You desire her to be as comfortable as possible in her last year (perhaps more?) of life. Creating conflict and introducing bad news works against this. You should lie to your grandmother and give her positive news because this action will provide to her the highest quality and quantity of life. [17]

Moral imperative: Lying is immoral. In cases in which one lies for his own sake it is deeply embedded. In cases in which one lies only for the sake of another, it is embedded in a surface manner.

One ought not to act paternalistically toward the sick. This is because you are not recognizing their basic human rationality. However, this is a prima facie rule that can be overridden by circumstances. In this case letting Granny be fully informed about her condition would not permit her free and unfettered choice. On the contrary, it would so agitate her that she might lose her mental coherence all together. Thus, the paternalism argument in this context is undetermined.

According to this analysis we can construct the following chart.

IMPERATIVE/Level of Embeddedness:	SURFACE	MEDIUM	DEEP
Prudential duty to Granny			X
Moral duty concerning lying	X		
Moral duty concerning autonomy		undetermined	

If I am correct in my assessment of relative embeddedness, then the prudential good that can accrue from boosting Granny's spirits by lying to her outweighs the moral sanctions against lying and paternalism (undetermined in this context since it cuts both ways). This is because the prudential imperative is more deeply embedded in this situation than is the moral imperative.

Some might contend that since lying and respect of human dignity are basic goods that they should be listed as deeply embedded. I have resisted this in the above case because in the first instance (lying) the protagonist is not lying to promote his own interests. He is lying for the sake of another's happiness (Granny's). Thus the essential feature that makes lying immoral (i.e., unfairly promoting one's own advantage at the expense of another) has been eliminated. To lie is to "freely say that which is untrue with the intent of deceiving another." But what makes lying unethical is when it is done for the sake of self-gain. Because deception is always an "action-limiting" event relative to the other agent (to some degree) and because the basis of moral goods relates to action, lying is never totally innocuous. This means that we shouldn't lie willy-nilly even in cases that do not promote self-interest. However, when there is a deeply embedded prudential interest at stake and the lie does not promote self-interest, then lying is permitted.

In the second case, paternalism is sanctioned because it denies the agent the free power to be involved in important decisions affecting him. However, in example 4 lying actually facilitates the empowering of Granny by letting her live in hope and not be subject to her known propensity to obsessively worry and become almost pathologically agitated. Granting unreflective autonomy will actually work against autonomy. It is thus undetermined. This whole evaluation revolves around a particular understanding of Granny. If she were a different sort of woman, the entire case and its resulting chart of embeddedness would be different.

The Burden of Proof

In the last section I suggested that using the concept of relative embeddedness is a way that we can measure complicated moral situations. However, it should be clear to everyone that this theory invites a grave danger. This danger arises when an agent is faced with a moral situation in which the prudential goods are deeply embedded and there is an ethical issue at stake. If the prudential good potentially benefits the agent in question, then he is sorely tempted to minimize the embeddedness of the moral dimension so that he might enjoy the prudential good.

Obviously, this is a problem. If the assigning of moral embeddedness is merely at the whim of the agent, then ethics breaks down and what we are left with is bald egoism. However, this need not be the case. *This is because there is a prima facie rule that in cases in which there exists an ethical dimension, ethical imperatives trump prudential imperatives.* In order to overturn this rule, one must demonstrate that there is an unequal embeddedness favoring the prudential imperative. Thus, the burden of proof is upon the agent to justify her attribution of surface or medium embeddedness to a given imperative within a situational construct.

How does one go about justifying a lesser-level attribution? This is largely an assessment of the consequences—not so as to add up utilities, but to incorporate these in one's description of the action. Once this is accomplished, one can determine how close to fundamental action the moral good in question is. If the good is basic to human action, then it will always be deeply embedded (unless there are other circumstances that would alter the character of the good).[18] If the good is secondary to human action, then it will always be trumped by a more highly embedded prudential good. Thus, in a time of war a commanding officer may treat some of his men with some disrespect (even though respecting humanity is a basic good) in order to get the job done because the consequences are life or death for the platoon. If the platoon leader's only way to get Private Smith to move forward is to curse at him, and if Smith's actions can save the lives of his platoon members, then a curse is permitted. (One might rank a curse in such circumstances as a minor instance of not respecting one's humanity. More serious violations might include those that occur over time—such as a factory manager who makes his workers toil in terrible conditions and for a wage beneath the prevailing pay.)

I could go on, but the point is clear that unless one creates a compelling case, based upon proximity to human action, that a moral good should be reranked—it will not be reranked. From a prima facie vantage point, the moral ranking of goods remains intact unless there is a compelling reason (based upon expected consequences that would cause us to reclassify the action in *this particular instance*).

Likewise, prudential goods should not be *overvalued*. As I have mentioned earlier, prudential goods should be judged on utilitarian terms using some reasonable version of cost-benefit analysis. This means that there will always be a limit on any individual's particular interests. If we accept Bentham's dictum that each person should count as one, then there will always be a limit to how much to weigh an individual's preferences.

This of course is not a full-blown moral theory, but is rather the outline of one. Along with the Personal Worldview Imperative and the Shared Community Imperative, it suggests a direction in which moral inquiry might proceed.

Notes

1. One need not go far to prove this point. In the Second World War the sieges of Leningrad and Stalingrad were poignant examples of people pressed at the level of basic goods (level one), see Anthony Beevor, *Stalingrad: The Fateful Siege, 1942-43* (New York: Penguin, 1999) and Harrison Evans Salisbury, *The 900 Days: The Siege of Leningrad* (New York: Da Capo Press, 1985). Of course there are also the horrific conditions in the Nazi concentration camps (see Zygmunt Bauman, *Modernity and the Holocaust* (Ithaca, New York: Cornell University Press, 1989)) and unfortunately many more. Even at the writing of this book millions around the world suffer the loss of level-one basic goods daily.

2. The notion of goods and action is one that deserves a treatment of its own. For the genesis of this concept as related to morality I am following Alan Gewirth, *Reason and Morality* (Chicago: University of Chicago Press, 1978), 53-58. I have extended the concept of how the classes are to be arranged somewhat particularly in the context of justice; see Michael Boylan, "Justice, Community, and the Limits of Autonomy," in *Social and Political Philosophy: Contemporary Perspectives,* ed. James P. Sterba (London: Routledge, 2001).

3. I am, of course, assuming that strange situations do not obtain, such as a person who needs to listen to music all the time or he will go into a coma or another such serious medical problem. The assumption here is that music is a pleasant but nonessential element to have available at all times. As such it is remotely connected to the ability to commit effective action.

4. The sense of "fairness" here relates to a theory of deserts. This is beyond the perimeters of this treatment. However, it appears rather clear that no one chooses her race. Thus, being of a particular race should not be held against someone. It is unfair to penalize anyone for that which is not a direct consequence of some action she has committed. Discriminating against African Americans in the United States is thus unfair. Since the consequences of this discrimination are not life-enhancing, it trumps all other secondary-good claims. For a fine discussion of different senses of "desert" see Louis P. Pojman and Owen McLeod, eds., *What Do We Deserve? A Reader on Justice and Desert* (New York: Oxford University Press, 1999).

5. The line between basic and secondary goods is set by the ability of an agent to act in a very objective way within a society. The line between life-enhancing, useful, and luxurious goods is less precise. It will probably vary over time and is certainly relative. Thus, this discussion must be a part of an ongoing discussion which each society should continually update.

6. The argument here is that human agency is fundamental to our human nature. It is that which all would claim above all else. If this is correct, and if there is a correlative duty between a moral rights claim and a collective duty, then all

would have a duty to provide each agent within the society with the two levels of basic agency. For a further discussion of this see Michael Boylan, *Basic Ethics* (Upper Saddle River, NJ: Prentice Hall, 2000), chapter 8.

7. It seems to me that luxury goods themselves can be broken into several classes rated according to the amount of societal resources/money required to convey this good. Thus, a compact disc music player is a luxury good at a relative low level since the cost is between $50 and $250 (at this writing). A yacht would be a rather high-level luxury good pricing between $750,000 and $10,000,000 (and up!).

8. There is, of course, the standard debate here about pleasure vs. happiness. I do not examine it in the body of the text because the parameters of happiness are contained in my depiction of morality and professionalism. For a discussion of this debate see Robert Nozick and his discussion of the "experience machine" in *Anarchy, State, and Utopia* (New York: Basic Books, 1974), 42-45; and concerning the problem as it is turned toward mental states see James Griffin, *Well-Being* (Oxford: Clarendon Press, 1986), chapter 1, and, of course, the classic treatment by Sigmund Freud, "On Narcissism: An Introduction," in Freud, *Collected Papers* (New York: Basic Books, 1959), vol. 4, 30-59.

9. It should be noted here that I have a rather broader concept of professions than some often provide. If one has a well-defined set of practices and an enforcement mechanism to legally define malpractice (unprofessional conduct), then I am content with calling the métier a profession. For a further discussion see Michael Boylan, *Basic Ethics* (Upper Saddle River, NJ: Prentice Hall, 2000), chapter 7.

10. This is a rather difficult imperative. Galen himself is said to have violated this dictum in the plague that afflicted Rome. In our own day, HIV and AIDS have brought this principle to the fore.

11. Obviously I am not examining all possible conflicts. Kierkegaard has written in *Fear and Trembling* that the ethical and the religious may conflict (as in the case of the Abraham and Isaac narrative). For Kierkegaard, the religious imperative supersedes the ethical imperative in such instances. I assume that other fundamental conflicts can occur in aesthetics as well. A more comprehensive treatment of such cases must be reserved for a future study.

12. For me these terms are synonymous. "Ethics" comes from the Greek and "morality" comes from the Latin—some say coined by Cicero while he was in exile, as a translation of the Greek term.

13. Here I am thinking of the standard act-utilitarian doctrines as adopted by Bentham, Mill, and Sidgwick: Jeremy Bentham, *An Introduction to the Principles of Morals and Legislation* (Oxford: Oxford University Press, 1789); John Stuart Mill, *Utilitarianism* (London: Parker, Son, and Bourny, 1863); Henry Sidgwick, *The Methods of Ethics,* 7th ed. (London: Macmillan, 1907). Of course, there have been many modifications to this traditional account. Some of

these include: David Lyons, *Rights, Welfare, and Mill's Moral Theory* (Oxford: Oxford University Press, 1994); Robert Merrihew Adams, "Motive Utilitarianism," *Journal of Philosophy* 73:14 (August 12, 1976): 467-81; Alan Gibbard, "Utilitarianism and Human Rights," *Social Philosophy and Policy* 1:2 (1984): 92-102; Donald Regan, *Utilitarianism and Co-operation* (Oxford: Clarendon Press, 1980); Michael Slote, *Common Sense Morality and Consequentialism* (London: Routledge, 1985); J. J. C. Smart and Bernard Williams, *Utilitarianism: For and Against* (Cambridge: Cambridge University Press, 1973).

14. Obviously there are cases of graft and corruption that will subvert this model. But the general model still obtains.

15. "Embedded" in this context means the relative fundamental nature of the good for action. A more deeply embedded good is one that is more primary to action.

16. I have mentioned health care (as a means to attaining health) as a basic good—thus incurring the correlative duty of society to provide the same—in my essay, "The Universal Right to Healthcare," in *Medical Ethics,* Michael Boylan, ed. (Upper Saddle River, NY: Prentice Hall, 2000), 391-402.

17. Of course this example and all the examples cited in this book might work differently if new information or new narrative perspectives are inserted. For the pedagogical interests of this example let us assume that only this information (or other facts consonant with this) exists, and let us leave opaque (meaning it has no moral significance) the narrative perspectives of unnamed characters.

18. The obvious exception to this would be when a good listed (such as lying) does not meet all the stated functional requirements, e.g., the lie is not for one's own sake but solely for the sake of another.

Chapter 6
Ethics in Professional Education

There are three arenas of moral decision making and higher education where students encounter ethical challenges and need to engage the process of ethical reflection—in the personal lives of each student, in the disciplines that shape the curriculum in which students learn, and in education in the professional schools of the university where students are introduced to the concepts, norms, and practices of professional life. This chapter analyzes the dynamics of the ethics of professional education and provides a model for developing an approach to teaching ethics in professional schools.

To become a professional is to enter a moral world constituted by a particular set of values and norms that circumscribe the kind of activities that occur in the profession of which one is a part.[1] To enter into a professional school is at one level to become educated in the knowledge and techniques that make a profession what it is. It is to learn the body of knowledge and the set of skills required to carry out the practices that identify and define the profession itself. Legal education is learning what constitutes the various aspects of the law and requires developing the knowledge sufficient to become a certified practicing attorney. Nursing education introduces the student to the information, knowledge, and training that will enable the successful graduate to fully engage in the practice of nursing. Engineering education gives students the knowledge and skills to construct and build systems that will deliver the forms and structures adequate to meet the needs and demands of a world that is built on principles of design. The foundation of all professional education is a body of knowledge and information that the profession itself and the society in which the profession is practiced determine as intrinsic to the profession.

Professional education, however, is more than simply the gaining of knowledge and technique. It is also an introduction to the moral framework that serves as the basis for the profession. Every profession manifests a set of values and norms that communicate an understanding of what is considered to be good, important, and worthwhile in the conduct of professional practice. Professions are based on a set of beliefs about what constitutes the good, an understanding of how the profession seeks to preserve and advance the good or goods in a particular society, and what activities are seen to be consistent with advancing this idea of the good. In a profession, certain values and types of behaviors are understood to be appropriate and internal to the goods of the profession.[2] To act in accord with those standards is considered to be the right way to engage in professional practices. The point of this chapter is to indicate how professional education communicates not only the knowledge and skills that constitute the profession, but also the values and ideas of the good that are integral to a body of professional knowledge. Every profession has a particular way of understanding the moral life of the profession. The goal of professional education should be to give each prospective professional the ability to understand and reflect upon the moral basis of the profession. To be a morally good professional one must possess skills of moral reflection as well as the practical knowledge, information, and techniques that constitute the profession.

Some examples will illustrate this point. The profession of law is based on a fundamental idea about what the law is, what laws are essential to establish the necessary order or a sense of justice for a society, and how those legal professionals who are entrusted with the implementation of the law ought to act in their role as professionals. Such a view suggests that a certain body of laws best constitutes the "good order" of a society, and that there are certain ways that these laws are affected and preserved in a society. The task of the lawyer as professional is to come to know what activities and conduct are appropriate to uphold and preserve the law. Thus in the adversary system that undergirds our legal system, the lawyer comes to know not only what laws are, but also how the rule of law is to be implemented and given form in a society. Similarly, in business education the student in training is introduced to a body of facts and information about what constitutes a market economy and what functions are necessary to preserve and excel in the actualization of that economy. The idea of the good or goods in business education is one that captures the essential purposes and goals to which the practice of business is committed. This will entail some notion of the role the economic marketplace plays in an understanding of human flourishing. Nursing education is based on some inherent idea of what the function, purposes, and goals of nursing are and how they are constituted by an idea of how these are promoting of the human good as manifested in good health and the healing of the sick. Professional education in all settings is based on a set of assumptions and premises about the idea of the good that is constitutive of each profession itself.

It is important to realize that the role of the professional does not merely assume that the norms of justice, business, or nursing are set in a settled and agreed-upon way. To the contrary, much of professional training entails an introduction into a mode of inquiry that examines a set of given assumptions and explores modes of professional organization that will better realize a more just/prosperous/healthy society. Conflict and contention are built into much professional education in that students are invited to imagine the construction of a better professional system. There is continual analysis and constant change built into professional education that engages students in the contextual assessment of presumed perspectives.

Professions and the Idea of Ethos

The notion of ethos best captures the idea of the moral framework inherent in a profession. Each profession is constituted by an ethos that shapes and defines it, and it is the ethos of a profession to which a student in training in the profession is introduced in the course of professional education.

There are several ways of defining ethos that help us to understand how an ethos functions:

"An ethos is the web of values, meanings, purposes, expectations, obligations and legitimations that constitutes the operating norms of a culture in relation to a social entity."[3] (Max Stackhouse, *Ethics and the Urban Ethos*)

"An ethos is that mixture of moral norms embedded in a culture, the historical intentionality that guides and directs that culture, the existing practices of the culture at any particular time, the future possibilities that are projected and betrayed in the social give and take."[4] (Gibson Winter, *Elements for a Social Ethic*)

"A people's ethos is the tone, character, and quality of their life, its moral and aesthetic style and mood; it is the underlying attitude toward themselves and their world that life reflects. Their world view is their picture of the way things in sheer actuality are, their concept of nature, of self, of society."[5] (Clifford Geertz, *The Interpretation of Cultures*)

In each of these definitions, it is clear that an ethos is not reducible to one component part, nor is it possible to merely depict a moral culture in simplistic unnuanced ways. The idea of ethos suggests that any culture is the construct of a variety of forces and factors that together constitute an environment in which there are clearly identifiable patterns of action and practices that serve to organize that culture. There is a defined sense of right and wrong, of what is valued or not, of what actions are deemed appropriate or inappropriate. From the perspective of ethics the critical insight of the idea of ethos is that it is constructed by both descriptive and normative patterns of behavior; that is, an ethos tells us not only *what does go on* in a culture but also how that culture understands and defines *what ought to go on*. There is both a descriptive and normative dimension to the concept of ethos.[6] An ethos tells us both what actually does exist in a group or society and what ought to exist, at least through the set of eyes that see the culture from the inside.

The claim of this analysis is that to enter a profession is to enter an ethos. It is to enter a world in which there are a set of values and beliefs that constitute the profession as it functions at this point in history. When one is educated and trained to be a professional, these values and beliefs are communicated to the trainee. There is an implicit form of moral education that goes on in professional education—an internalization of professional norms occurs.[7] The question of this study is whether the way this education takes place really captures an idea of the good that is adequate in that it can be justified and defended under critical scrutiny. An adequate understanding of the goods of a profession must be justified on grounds that are not only internal to the profession but also are defensible according to criteria that have some objectifiable grounding.

The goal of ethics education across the curriculum in professional schools is to introduce students to what it means to be a member of a profession and to the moral world which the student is entering. It is at the same time to give the student the analytic skills to critically assess the ethos structures of a profession and to make determinations about practices and professional decisions that are consistent with critically held and defensible understandings of what is good action for human persons. It is at this point that the classic theories of ethical analysis—utility, justice, rights, and virtue—provide a comprehensive critical basis for assessing a professional ethos and professional decisions. Professions are structured to deliver a set of functions in a given society. The ethics of the professions requires an understanding of what goods the profession is to deliver and what decisions, values, and practices are consistent with those goods. One way of summarizing the task of ethics in professional schools is that it is to introduce students to a critical understanding of ethos.

The Components and Carriers of an Ethos

For the professional in training it is imperative to understand the ways that an ethos is communicated and how a professional can detect the content of the moral meanings of an ethos. Again, there is no singular way that an ethos is conveyed. Rather, it is contained in the multiple meanings and values that are expressed in a variety of organizational practices. These include:

Organizational structures—by the way an organization is structured and by how patterns of authority and priority are communicated and defined. Whether an organization is hierarchical or horizontal will be indicative of the way that decisions are made, the level of input and authority that various organizational members have and are allowed to have, and who or what is valued. Values, and appropriate ways of practicing the business of the organization, will be reflected in how an organization is constructed. Military organizations, for example, place a high priority on a chain-of-command type of decision-making and authority. Consumer organizations, by contrast, manifest a very participatory organizational structure where all members of the organization equally share decisions and authority. The ethos of each type of organization will be different. The appropriate type of organizational structure is shaped in large measure by the goods, purposes, and functions of the organization.

Leadership—by the way that the leaders of an organization communicate what is valuable and important in the organization and profession. Who is "in charge" and what that person communicates will be vital for understanding the ethos of an organization or profession. Every profession has its exemplars, those who embody the essential values and models of success and greatness for the profession. It makes a great difference who these models of success are and what they communicate in terms of what it valuable and important in the conduct of the activity of the profession.

Role specification—by the responsibilities that are spelled out in the formal and informal job descriptions of professionals. When one takes a position as a professional in an organization there is always a job description attached to the job. This will spell out a range of actions and decisions that are expected and considered appropriate for effective functioning. The moral parameters of the professional will be shaped in some measure by the content of this job description.

Rituals, signs, and symbols of the profession and organization—by the values and expectations that are communicated in the events, both formal and informal, in which the members of an organization participate. The formal ceremonies of a profession—graduations and convocations in academic life, stockholder meetings in corporations, the rituals of trial practiced in the law—all communicate a sense of the important and valuable. The informal rituals of an organization—meetings by the coffee urn, volleyball at break time, happy hours after work—also communicate a sense of what is expected and allowed in organizational life. The messages communicated in these rituals are essential ingredients of ethos.

Codes of ethics—the values and beliefs that an organization or profession articulates as guiding principles for the work of those who are employed in the organization or are members of the profession. The principles and moral standards are typically developed by those internal to a profession after an occupational group has developed to a point where self-regulation, standards of membership, and criteria for censure are vital for the effective, and sometimes legal, development of the profession. These codes function as a framework for framing the ethical quality of professional conduct. It is hoped that these guiding values have been internalized in the practices and activities of those in the company and profession.

Organizational mission and purpose—the founding commitments and intentions, reasons for starting an organization, and the essential values of the founders of the company. These are frequently articulated from generation to generation as an institution develops and grows over time. It is not uncommon for the publications and communications of a company to have the values and beliefs of the company displayed prominently in official literature and discussed to some degree in employee orientation. Mission and purpose tell what the organization does in a general way and are used to frame the scope of activities, product lines, and the generic range of activities that are deemed appropriate for the profession. Lawyers do not engage in medical work; manufacturing companies are not social-service providers (although they may provide some services to their employees); nurses are not civil engineers. While these demarcations may be obvious, the articulation of organizational mission is an important directional marker for what companies and professions do, and what those who use their services can expect in their interaction with the professional.

An ethos is a composite of all of these features and identifying traits. Ethics education is crucial for the student in training to develop the skills to be able to detect the moral messages and meanings contained in these indicators and to be able to make discriminating and critical judgments about professional action based on them. In some professions (especially the helping professions) transmission of values is explicit and very intentional.

The Moral Responsibilities of the Professional

The idea of professional ethics is rooted in a fundamental understanding of what a profession is and what a professional does. Professions are occupational groups that are formed to perform a particular service in a society or to carry out a particular function.[8] By virtue of the kind of service that is performed and in light of the requirements for carrying out the functions necessary, a set of attributes are ascribed to the professional. Historically the professions have been restricted to those occupational groups that would provide a service to others or to a community and there was little or no self-interest or reward associated with the service. This of course has changed over the course of history. A very vigorous debate goes on in professional circles today as to whether the defining characteristic of professional identity is based on principles of altruism or self-interest.[9]

There are certain essential qualities that define the profession and the professional. The professional is one who:

- Is engaged in a social service that is essential and unique;
- Has developed a high degree of specialized knowledge;
- Has developed the ability to apply the special body of knowledge to the profession;
- Is part of a group that is autonomous and claims the right to regulate itself;
- Recognizes and affirms a code of ethics;
- Exhibits strong self-discipline and accepts personal responsibility for actions and decisions;
- Is committed and concerned with the communal self-interest rather than the self;

- Is more concerned with services rendered rather than with financial rewards.[10]

This definition serves as an ideal type rather than a checklist for membership in the professions. As is obvious, the critical issues concern the degree to which the professional acts in the service of others or is motivated by self-interest and gain.

Since the professional has the ability to affect and influence the lives of clients or customers in a significant way, the professional and the professions rely on some fundamental sense of trust that serves as the basis for the successful relationships and decisions among professionals and those they serve. Since professionals possess knowledge that is "dangerous" in that the specialized information is not known to those that are served and it can be used in ways that can be harmful to people, professions and professionals can be successful only when there is sufficient trust that exists within the profession.[11] Professionals therefore possess a fiduciary responsibility to those they serve to use their knowledge and expertise in ways that are constructive and helpful for what is humanly good. Actions or decisions by the professional that erode this confidence and trust are clearly ethically deficient.

Role Morality in the Professions

When an individual seeks out a professional for his or her services the dynamics of the exchange shape the moral responsibilities that are at play in the interaction. The one seeking assistance comes to the professional because he or she possesses information that the client needs to achieve some end or goal.[12] The professional is trained in the knowledge and functioning of the service, an expertise that the client does not have him or herself. The client has confidence that the information that is needed will be given in accord with basic assumptions and understandings about what the profession is and the role that it plays in the life of the society. Lawyers are experts in the law, doctors are experts in some areas of health that are hopefully curative, engineers have the expertise of design and structure that will help to achieve structures and processes necessary for the physical operation of a society's well-being. The client is dependent on the knowledge the professional possesses. The professional in turn has the ability to affect constructive or destructive ends with the knowledge he or she possesses. There are basic assumptions about trust and the constructive use of the information that is being sought and the professional's delivery of that knowledge that are essential for a coherent understanding of what professions are. It is these very assumptions that are filled with values and understandings of the good that shape the way that the ethics of the professions are to be understood. The moral norms and directions for professional action are rooted in the structural goals and purposes of the profession itself.

Ethics as Internal and External to the Professions

The obvious critique that can be raised about the ethical analysis at this point is how to assure that the moral justification for professional decisions is based on more than simply a self-referencing notion of what appears to be good from the perspective of one who is inside the tradition or profession.[13] On what basis does one ground an ethic to assure that it is defensible as more than merely self-interest or illusory notions of the good? The answer to this dilemma requires a set of moral justifications that address both the subjective and objective claims of morality. The claim of this argument is that professional decisions can be ethically justified only on grounds that satisfy conceptual conditions that derive from a fundamental understanding about human reasoning and logical analysis. It is also the contention here that the interplay between the classic philosophical theories of Western ethical analysis provides a justificatory framework that can be used for making ethical decisions in the professions. Introducing students to these modes of moral justification and providing a framework in which they are interrelated to form a holistic moral framework is an important goal for ethics across the curriculum in professional schools.[14]

Concepts of Utility

1. Almost all ethical thinking involves anticipating the *consequences* of alternative courses of action. As least one aspect of ethical actions, most thinkers believe, is that they bring about good and minimize harm to others.

Utilitarianism is a theory about ethics which says that, in fact, considerations of consequences are more than *one* feature of ethical thinking—they are the whole of it.[15] In general, utilitarian thinking says those acts are right which bring about the greatest good for the greatest number of affected parties (stakeholders) in the action, or which minimize the harms to others.

2. *Cost-benefit analysis.* Although utilitarianism has been around for several hundred years as an ethical theory, it has taken on a mathematically precise form in the use of cost-benefit analysis in modern economics. Much public policy discussion rests on such analysis, and there is an important moral component to such use: the attempt to make sure the resources are spent rationally and with the greatest efficiency. Cost-benefit analysis raises critical questions, however—most of which apply to the entire utilitarian enterprise.

One major objection is that it requires quantifying costs and benefits with a degree of precision that many find dubious, and many more find morally offensive. The value of a human life, for example, may turn out to be assessed by determining the economic discounted future earnings the person would have acquired had he lived.

Another objection is that consequentialist thinking is always "forward-looking," and tends to discount "backward-looking" moral considerations such as promise keeping, friendship and family obligations, etc.

A third objection focuses on the unpredictability of the future and the problem of setting the relevant time-framework within which to think about the consequences (i.e., how far "out" should one think things through; short-term benefit may turn into long-term cost).

3. *Practical applications of utility.* In practical ethics, most of us would agree that utility considerations need to be balanced with other types of ethical considerations such as *rights* and *justice*. Each of these types of issues can be thought of as a "vector"—a single dimension of a situation which *tends* to make something right or wrong, but which must include the other vectors in order to make an overall moral assessment.

Concepts of Rights
1. In the broadest sense a *right* is a *justified claim*. Both words are important. "Claims" are liberties or goods an individual asserts he or she should have. Some of these claims are valid; some are not. "Rights-talk" invites us to inquire into the justifications offered for that claim. Hence, *right* = *justified* claim.[16]

2. *Justifications.* There are varieties of rights, each differentiated from the others on the basis of the nature of the justifications.

One category is *positive rights.* These are rights which one has by virtue of some socially designated rule or social status. For example, federal employees have certain rights *because* those rights are enumerated in various laws and policies governing federal employment. For positive rights, the justification required is that there is some law, rule, or perhaps even custom which says that right exists.

Another type of rights is *natural*. The Declaration of Independence, for example, refers to the "self-evident" truths that "all men are created equal, and endowed by their Creator with certain inalienable rights; that among these are life, liberty, and the pursuit of happiness." For this type of right, note that the justification required is an appeal to human nature generally, to the dignity of human beings and their moral status. Of course, it is a deep question to what extent such claims can be justified, and an even deeper one to attempt to work out the justification.

3. *Liberty/Entitlement rights.* Another set of contrast terms divide up rights concepts into two categories: liberty and entitlement.

Liberty rights are rights individuals have to do things without interference by other individuals or by the government. Examples are the major constitutional rights: assembly, religious practice, speech, etc. In the American tradition, this is the category of rights most deeply embedded in our political and philosophical tradition.

Entitlement rights are justified claims an individual makes on social goods or services. Clearly there are legally established entitlements such as governmentally provided income during periods of unemployment.

Many controversial issues in our society turn on philosophical questions regarding these two types of rights. Supreme Court rulings (at least up to the present) have said there is a *negative right* to abortion (the state may not interfere with a woman's decision to have an abortion), but that there is *no positive right* (entitlement) to abortion—the state is not required to provide abortion to indigent women if it chooses not to.

4. *Correlativity thesis.* This is a thesis about the logic of rights, which may or may not be true. It claims that for every right one person has, another identifiable person or group has an *obligation* which is correlative to that right. For example, if Jean has a right to free speech, each of us has a moral obligation with respect to Jean's right—not improperly to interfere with her speaking.

With negative or liberty rights, this thesis seems to hold fairly straightforwardly: all others have obligations with respect to an individual's liberty rights, viz., to respect them. There is a problem with entitlement rights and the correlativity thesis, however: it's harder, and maybe impossible, to point to which individuals and groups have obligations with respect to them. So if there's a right to food, say, whose obligation is it to provide food? What if there simply aren't enough resources to provide food to everyone?

Concepts of Distributive Justice[17]

1. *Distributive justice.* A primary concern of ethics education is *distributive* justice—the principle that guides our thinking about the allocation of social goods and services. Questions of distributive justice arise whenever there are more demands and wants for a particular thing than there is availability of it. In broad terms, when we ask the distributive justice question we are asking what allocation of such resources would be "fair."

2. *Formal justice.* In the abstract (formally), justice is easy to define. Classical definitions are the following: "Equals [in the morally relevant respects] should be treated equally" or "To each his/her due." Such phrases capture accurately and concisely our moral intuitions about abstract justice. But of course they are empty of "material" (i.e., intellectually specific and substantive) content. They leave aside entirely the question of which groups and individuals really are equal "in the morally relevant respects." They do not tell us the morally substantive thing: what really is "due" to each?

3. *Material criteria of justice.* If the formula for formal justice is "Equals [in the morally relevant respects] should be treated equally," material criteria of justice are meant to tell us what constitutes such morally relevant respects. If formal justice's formula is "To each his/her due," material criteria are needed to flesh out such an abstract formula and to specify a criterion to determine what *is* due to each.

4. *Alternative material criteria of justice.* The following is a list of some material criteria of distributive justice:

- To each person an equal share,
- To each person according to that person's need,
- To each person according to that person's effort,
- To each person according to that person's contribution,
- To each person according to that person's merit,
- To each person according to that person's exchanges.

5. *Which criterion to apply?* The serious work of a theory of justice is, of course, to help us determine which of these criteria, singly or in combination, is appropriate in a particular allocational situation. About some allocations we're pretty clear. Automobiles, for example, are allocated on the basis of free-market exchanges, and few find this problematic morally. Rhodes scholarships are allocated on the basis of merit as measured

by clear and uniform criteria of merit, and that seems unproblematic too. Pieces of a child's birthday cake are allocated on the basis of equality (and usually a procedure like "she who cuts gets the last slice" is instituted to insure that outcome!).

Other allocations are less clear. On what basis *is* health care presently allocated? The answer is a very complex mix of these criteria. On what basis *should* health care be allocated? On this we have no social consensus.

6. *Theories of justice.* Theories of justice are meant to guide our thinking in areas (like health care and employment) where social practice and consensus is confused or nonexistent. Some of the dominant contemporary theories include:

Utilitarian—Justice requires the most stringent forms of obligation created by the principle of utility. Emphasis is on political planning to bring about justice, defined as the greatest good for the greatest number.

Libertarian—Central emphasis on individual liberty and personal rational choice. Any allocation that results from the free, informed, and uncoerced choices of all participants is by definition just. In practice, libertarian theories tend to stress the unfettered free markets as the essential mechanism for equitable distribution of goods in the society.

Rawlsian/Egalitarian—Egalitarian theories stress an absolutely equal distribution of social goods. John Rawls' very influential *A Theory of Justice* departs somewhat from strict egalitarianism, allowing inequality according to a strict test: does the inequality benefit the least well-off in the society (by providing incentive for the talented to work very hard, thereby increasing the aggregate social resources, for example)? The theoretical derivation of this principle comes from a hypothetical situation of free and disinterested agents choosing behind a "veil of ignorance" regarding the actual status in the society they design.

7. *Fair opportunity rule.* What is the line between the unfair/unjust and the merely unfortunate when it comes to the "natural lottery" of burdens individuals bear? If race, sex, physical and mental disabilities, etc. distinguish individuals, what does justice require regarding those differences? The fair opportunity rule states (controversially, of course) that individuals should not be penalized, and should be compensated to the maximum extent possible, for burdens they bear for which they are not responsible.

Concepts of Virtue/Traits of Character

1. *Virtue* is a term which, in modern parlance, may seem quaint or outdated. It is, however, the best term we have in English to label an important moral reality. "Virtue" comes from the Latin *virtus,* meaning "strength." It designates those strengths of character that enable a person to fulfill his or her duties, even in difficult circumstances or adversity. Since Aristotle, philosophers have noted that rational training in moral thinking alone is inadequate to develop these strengths. Rather, proper upbringing, frequent practice of the skills required, and the company and encouragement of friends and colleagues who encourage and model noble conduct are needed for such powers to be fully nurtured. As such, virtues are a kind of *habit*—a settled disposition to act in desirable ways.[18]

2. *Integrity.* At root, "integrity" stems from the Latin *integer,* "whole." The virtue of integrity describes that state of personal wholeness in which our lives and choices are consistent with the values and principles we affirm intellectually. Integrity is compromised whenever we make exceptions to our principles for reasons of expediency or personal advancement.

3. *Honesty.* The virtue of honesty refers most obviously to not lying. But there are more subtle aspects of the virtue as well. For example, while "lying" refers most clearly to direct and intentional statement of untruths, there are various shades of the deviation from this virtue. For example, dissimulation is the intentional misleading of another party, even if it does not directly involve lying. Of course, nothing requires telling another everything one thinks—some have defined honesty as "telling others what they have a right to know." It is a violation of the conduct that would flow from this virtue when others are not told what they have a right to know.

4. *Trustworthiness.* Trustworthiness is the virtue that allows us to have confidence in another. To trust someone is to place something of crucial importance to us in their hands, and to believe that it is reposed with them safely. To be trustworthy is to be prepared to accept and to be worthy of others' reliance upon us.

5. *Virtues and moral principles* (such as justice, rights, and utility). Virtues are adjectives we apply to *persons;* moral principles we apply to *actions.* Yet there is a deep and necessary connection between them. Only those who possess moral virtues can be relied upon to act consistently on moral principle. How such virtues are formed and sustained is a deep philosophical and psychological question. The fundamental job of

moral leadership is to create a professional environment where action on principle is expected, rewarded, and fostered, and in which cynicism about the consequences of right action is not allowed to grow.

Using the Classic Theories
Each of these modes of moral justification can exist on its own as a way of defending one's moral claims. Most moral justifications are constructed by blending these theories. The weaknesses of each approach are corrected through the appropriation of another perspective to address the deficiencies. For example, rights theory provides a basis for correcting the potential for an "easy utilitarian" justification that might justify too much for the greatest good.

The issue being addressed for which resolution is sought typically determines which theory to employ or what composite of these theories to employ. The issue recommends the moral justification rather than the theory dictating the "right" solution. James Gustafson, in his work on justification, indicates that in most situations the best ethical theory (and choice) is the one that addresses the particular needs set forth by the issue.[19] This is not to be construed as a situation ethics approach but rather as an indication that good ethics derives from an ability to help resolve real issues and conflicts.

Professional Ethics and the Ethos of
Democratic Liberalism

The ethics of the professions in American society and culture cannot be understood independent of an analysis of their context in the ethos of democratic liberalism, the prevailing social and cultural identity of this nation. The organizing insights of our political association are based on a common belief in a set of values and on an agreement about how those values serve as the organizing principles for our common life. Both the embedded values and shared community worldviews approaches to ethics across the curriculum assume that there resides in our common life a set of values that are manifested in the interactions that constitute our common life, including the activities of the profession. The tenets of liberalism help identify both the embedded and shared values at work in our common life. The analysis of liberalism and its strengths and weaknesses also displays the major fault lines in our common moral thinking.

The idea of liberalism is made up of three interrelated parts: a theory of politics and society, a theory of human nature, and a view of reason.[20] Political and social associations derive primarily from the idea of the individual, conceived independently of social relationships. Political life is the aggregate collective of atomic, self-interested individuals who come together for the sake of achieving ends as driven by individual passions and interests. The idea of reason in liberalism is captured by the scientific understanding of knowledge as the "power to analyze and recombine elements for the sake of control and order."[21] Reason is instrumental in that it is to be used as the mechanism for achieving ends. Whether the ends are the goals of self- or collective interests is one of the interesting moral issues in political liberalism.

The values of liberty and freedom, and the rights that individuals have to these values, are the essential features of political liberalism. Our social arrangements are meant to advance the idea that we as individuals and as groups can construct a common life together and build the institutions and structures necessary to advance this life. Liberalism is built on the fundamental belief that each individual possesses a particular conception of the good and that the purpose of our social structures is to create a common life that enables individuals to pursue their particular notions of the good to the maximal extent possible (to the point where the extension of one's freedom interferes with the freedom of another individual). The role of the state and government is to oversee those common resources and practices that are necessary to enable common life to function. These include the basic services of schooling, police, maintenance of public property, and other essential services.

The contemporary challenge to liberal democratic systems concerns their ability to create a sufficient degree of consensus and community to prevent the tendency to individualism in a system that is built on the premise that the social good is derivative of the individual good. Social critics have accused liberalism of creating a culture of individualism in that the bonds of community are attenuated and stressed in times when there are limited social resources or extensive pluralism and diversity among peoples, ethnicities, religions, and subcultures in a particular culture.[22] The dominant tension in social analysis that defines our time is the tension between communitarianism and individualism.

Communitarians argue for social structures and policies that will create a sense of solidarity among individuals in that the primary unit of social, political, and moral analysis is the individual—understood in an intrinsically social sense, that is. The individual is not prior to the society of which he or she is a part, but rather, self and other are seen as an integral unit. Communitarians criticize liberalism for its individualistic roots, which they claim lead inevitably to excessive individualism and self-interest.

The discussion between communitarianism and liberalism reflects some of the basic issues and conflicts in professional ethics that have been developed in this analysis of ethics across the curriculum. The embedded values approach and the idea of ethos both are premised on the idea that values are at play in all that we do at both a personal and social level. This is fundamentally a descriptive claim in that it contends that all we do is value-laden and that if one is to do a serious analysis of the moral life, it is necessary to understand which values are at work and how they interact in the situation under analysis. The shared community worldview approach suggests that there are basic requirements of common life that lead to the moral imperative that the conditions of common life need to be developed.

Our approach to professional ethics across the curriculum is premised on the assertion that there exist fundamental basic rights and freedoms that have a primacy in the moral life and that essential to the work of ethics across the curriculum is the need to create a mode of analysis in university curricula that will examine the nature of these rights and goods, and that the reasoning process for making the case for them be coherent and compelling. This is not to suggest that ideas of utility, social contract, virtue and justice theories are not integral to the creation of a moral system but only that the system contain an adequate notion of rights and their corollary responsibilities.

The Social Context of Professional Ethics

The professions in modern society are a construct of our social and political situation, and the goals and purposes of the professions in a liberal democratic society provide the organizing framework for understanding professional life. The ethical conflicts of the professions are in large measure reflections of the tensions and conflicts that permeate the larger social ethos. The paradigmatic examples of these are the tensions between self-interest and the common good in the lives of the professional. Some examples illustrate the correlation between these arenas of social conflict.

Legal Ethics. The legal system in this country is based on the fact that citizens possess rights that are protected by the state and through the courts. The role of the attorney in this system is to be the protector and advocate of these rights. This is done through the zealous advocacy of the client's rights in an adversarial system that presumes that the competing rights of the plaintiff or defendant are balanced through the zealous advocacy of a competing attorney. The conceptual presumption in our legal system is that through this process an objective and truthful rendering of a verdict of justice will emerge.

Many of the ethical conflicts that arise in the field of law are the outgrowth of the tensions that are deeply embedded in this legal system: the conflict between an individual's rights and the collective good; the extent to which advocacy becomes invasive of the rights of the individual; the propensity to resolve disputes through litigation and adversarial positioning rather than through less aggressive means of resolution; and the presumption that the common good will arise through a process of advancing an individual's rights against the collective. These are but a few examples of the kinds of issues that constitute the field of legal ethics that arise from the value tensions that are embedded in our social and political context.

Ethics education[23] in a legal context must provide a framework of analysis adequate to address ethical conflicts internal to the profession. It must also provide an opportunity for law students to examine the underlying value assumptions that shape the legal profession and give a context for which assessment and judgment about these assumptions can be made. It ought ideally as well to give lawyers in training the opportunity to examine the socialization process that is at work for each student in the process of legal education.

Business Ethics. The tensions between autonomy and self-interest on the one hand and the common good or the collective well-being on the other are core tensions in both the ethos of democratic liberalism and in most ethical conflicts in business. A cursory glance at most popular texts in business ethics bears this out. The very premises of the free market system are based on a fundamental conviction that the advancement of individual self-interest (in the form of a product) in the market will be met with an appropriate level of response in the form of consumer demand to create a degree of profitability. The system itself is believed to provide the offsetting constraints to ultimately yield a balanced and fair system of exchange for all. While the complexities of the dynamics of market issues are considerable, the issue for business ethics education is to situate the fundamental ethical tensions in business in the context of the larger value assumptions of our social and political system.

Issues like conflict of interest in business, protection of consumer interests, the clash of business interests with the collective well-being, and issues of government regulation over business practices are representative of some of the major ethical conflicts in business. Each of these can best be understood and resolved by contextualizing them in the larger schema of the social and political ethos of which they are a part. It is this framework for ethical analysis that should constitute the context of an ethics across the curriculum program.

Ethics in the Health Care Professions. The issues of medical ethics have become quite well-known in both professional ethics circles and in the general public. While medical, nursing, and allied health sciences ethics are already developed fields in the academy, the dominant method of analysis typically posits a set of moral norms and principles and analyzes cases in the context of those principles. The approach advanced here is one that connects these principles to their roots in the ethos of democratic liberalism. Such a framework will give fuller content and depth to the students understanding of the moral dynamics at work in their chosen fields of study.

An example from one of the key texts in medical ethics will illustrate the point. In Beauchamp and Childress's classic text, *Principles of Biomedical Ethics,* the authors cite four basic norms as governing decisions in most ethical cases in medicine: autonomy, nonmaleficence, beneficence, and justice.[24] While these norms provide a helpful fundamental template for making ethical choices, they do not provide a nuanced framework of analysis that can enable decision makers to see the dynamics and background considerations of the larger ethos that are critical for effective moral choice. Ethics education that explicates the moral context for professional decisions is a necessary ingredient to enhancing the fabric of professional practice.

Notes

1. This view derives from an understanding of the idea of ethos as developed in the work of Max Stackhouse, *Ethics and the Urban Ethos: An Essay in Social Theory and Theological Construction* (Boston: Beacon Press, 1972); Gibson Winter, *Elements for a Social Ethic: Scientific and Ethical Perspectives on Social Process* (New York: Macmillan, 1966); Paul Camenisch, *Grounding Professional Ethics in a Pluralistic Society* (New York: Haven Publications, 1983).

2. This derives in large measure from Alasdair MacIntyre's idea of practices as developed in *After Virtue: A Study in Moral Theory* (Notre Dame, IN: University of Notre Dame Press, 1980).

3. Stackhouse, *Ethics and the Urban Ethos,* 5.

4. Winter, *Elements for a Social Ethic,* 218.

5. Clifford Geertz, *The Interpretation of Cultures: Selected Essays* (New York: Basic Books, 1973), 127.

6. For a fuller treatment of the descriptive-normative issue in ethics, see chapter 2.

7. The classic study on the topic is John Finley Scott, *The Internalization of Norms: A Sociological Theory of Moral Commitment* (Englewood Cliffs, NJ: Prentice-Hall, 1971).

8. The classic work on the issue is Talcott Parsons, "The Professions and Social Structure," *Social Forces* 17 (May 1939): 457-67.

9. This issue continues to be at the heart of the debate about ethics and the professions. See William May, *The Beleaguered Rulers: The Public Obligation of the Professional* (Louisville, KY: Westminster John Knox Press, 2001).

10. This typology is based on the work of Denis Campbell, *Doctors, Lawyers, Ministers: Christian Ethics in Professional Practice* (Nashville: Abingdon Press, 1982), 21-26.

11. The idea of the fiduciary responsibility of the professional is a central issue in professional ethics. See Stuart W. Herman, *Durable Goods: A Covenantal Ethics for Management and Employees* (Notre Dame, IN: University of Notre Dame Press, 1997).

12. For an analysis of the idea of role morality, see David Luban, ed., *The Good Lawyer: Lawyers' Roles and Lawyers' Ethics* (Totawa, NJ: Rowman and Allanheld, 1983). See especially the essays by Richard Wasserstrom, Virginia Held, and Susan Wolf.

13. This is the primary criticism made to proponents of a virtue approach to ethics. I am indebted to the respondents to a paper I (Donahue) gave, "A Virtue Approach to Ethics across the Curriculum," at Rochester Institute of Technology in October 1999, for sharpening my thinking on the point. See also Mark L. Cook, *The Open Circle: Confessional Method in Theology* (Minneapolis: Fortress Press, 1991).

14. The modes of moral justification outlined here are based on the writings of Martin L. Cook, prepared for and presented to an audience of Defense Department acquisition officers for a program entitled, "Teaching the Teachers of Defense Acquisition Officers." This program was co-directed by Dr. Cook and James Donahue and offered through the Department of Defense from 1990-1994.

15. The classic works in utilitarian ethics include John Stuart Mill and Jeremy Bentham, *Utilitarianism and Other Essays* (New York: Penguin Books, 1987).

For an overview of utilitarian theory, see William K. Frankena, *Ethics,* 2nd ed. (Englewood Cliffs, NJ: Prentice-Hall, 1973), 34-60.

16. For a comprehensive overview and analysis of rights and rights theory, see Ronald Dworkin, *Taking Rights Seriously* (Cambridge, MA: Harvard University Press, 1977); David Hollenbach, *Claims in Conflict: Retrieving and Renewing the Catholic Human Rights Tradition* (New York: Paulist Press, 1979); Michael Ignatieff et al., *Human Rights as Politics and Idolatry* (Princeton, NJ: Princeton University Press, 2001); David Lyons, *Rights* (Belmont, CA: Wadsworth Publishing, 1979); A. I. Melden, *Rights and Persons* (Berkeley: University of California Press, 1977); and W. D. Ross, *The Right and the Good* (Oxford: Clarendon Press, 1930).

17. John Rawls, *A Theory of Justice* (Cambridge, MA: Harvard University Press, 1971).

18. The concept of virtue is developed more fully in chapter 1.

19. In particular, see James Gustafson, "What is the Normatively Human?" in *Theology and Christian Ethics* (Philadelphia: United Church Press, 1974).

20. William M. Sullivan, *Reconstructing Public Philosophy* (Berkeley: University of California Press, 1982), 1-22.

21. Sullivan, *Reconstructing Public Philosophy,* 19.

22. The work of Robert Bellah is the most familiar contemporary analysis of the individual-communitarian debate. See *Habits of the Heart: Individualism and Commitment in American Life* (Berkeley: University of California Press, 1985). For an overview of communitarian theory see Amitai Etzioni, ed., *The Essential Communitarian Reader* (Lanham, MD: Rowman & Littlefield, 1998).

23. See Thomas Donaldson and Patricia H. Werhane, eds., *Ethical Issues in Business: A Philosophical Approach* (Englewood Cliffs, NJ: Prentice-Hall, 1979); Ronald M. Green, *The Ethical Manager: A New Method for Business Ethics* (New York: Macmillan College Publishing Company, 1994); Charles S. McCoy, *Management of Values: The Ethical Difference in Corporate Policy and Performance* (Boston: Pitman Publishing, Inc., 1985); and Manuel G. Velasquez, *Business Ethics: Concepts and Cases* (Englewood Cliffs, NJ: Prentice-Hall, 1982).

24. Tom L. Beauchamp and James F. Childress, *Principles of Biomedical Ethics* (New York: Oxford University Press, 1994).

Chapter 7
Religion and Other Values

The issue of the religious beliefs of students raises an important issue for understanding ethics across the curriculum, primarily because there is a commonly held belief that ethical choices are derived for many from religious convictions. Such a view contends that there is a logical and deductive process that translates religious beliefs and moral principles derived from them into ethical choices and decisions. This is a simplistic and reductionistic understanding.

The idea of what constitutes religious belief and the relationship between religion and ethics is the focus of this chapter. The analysis here relates the idea of the Personal Worldview Imperative to the issue of religion as it is presented in the university context. The Personal Worldview Imperative recognizes a process of self-analysis that will lead to the creation of a plan of life that is coherent, comprehensive, and good. This construction is associated with a religious worldview in that its scope and content frequently include dimensions of human experience that are typically identified as religious. Within the Personal Worldview Imperative, there is a recognition that basic aspects of human experience are central to our lives and are core to our existence: ethics, religion, spirituality, and aesthetics (among others). These are lived out in the context of social institutions and the cultural location in which we live, and become translated in a political/social arena through which (in democracies) public policy is formulated.

This chapter will sketch out first how religion and other core dimensions of human life are related to the personal worldview and then secondly how such recognition can be brought into a public arena through ethics across the curriculum.

Religion and Other Values

First, we will examine the way that religion and other modes of experience fit into the personal worldview. Then we will examine just how these might be accommodated by the Personal Worldview Imperative.

A. Faith, Theology, Beliefs: Some Basic Definitions

A full understanding of the role that religion plays in the discussion of
ethics across the curriculum requires first giving precision to terms that
are frequently interchanged in ways that are typically confused.

Both a religious and a philosophical perspective begin with the asking
of the basic questions about human existence; who am I/who are we/
what is the meaning of our existence?[1] It is this basic question of human
meaning that provides the departure point for our inquiry. To assert this
question as central is to claim that it is the core concern that each of us as
humans has and that as meaning-making creatures our lives are at root
attempts to give meaning and definition to this question. A *religious answer* to this question is one that asserts that a notion of God is decisive in
providing an adequate answer. To say that God is decisive is not necessarily to explain how or in which way God is decisive, but basically is to
establish that an adequate answer to the human question must entail
some fundamental affirmation about the reality of God. To speak of the
reality of God is to speak in some way of the necessity of a notion of
transcendence to provide adequate explanations for the basic human
question. It is important to realize that this definition in no way indicates
what substantive content provides the most adequate answer to the human question, only that it is answerable fully in light of some concept of
the divine, the ultimate, or the transcendent. The philosophical answer to
the human question is premised on the ability of reason alone to provide
adequate explanations to our questions.

Theology is the investigation that seeks to explain more fully the reality of God that is the fundamental premise in the religious answer to the
human question. The classical definition of theology is "faith seeking
understanding." This definition of St. Anselm refers to the attempt "to
make sense of" and to more fully understand the nature of some experience of the divine, either personal, communal, or historical, that calls out
to be more fully explicated and explained.

The findings of theology are explicated, organized, and systematized
in ways that lead to the formulation of particular beliefs. These are typically organized in concrete historical settings, or social organizations and
institutions that form traditions, churches, and religious bodies. These
traditions formulate beliefs, doctrines, and dogmas that serve to provide
a basis and framework for the expression of common commitments that
hold religious groups together. Each denomination or tradition will con-
cretize its understanding of the divine in ways that will issue in rules,

principles, and laws that serve as marks of distinction and demarcation that differentiate them from other religious expressions.

Religious traditions develop sets of values, moral standards, principles, rules, or laws that will frame the realm of appropriate behaviors in light of the explicated religious beliefs that are espoused in the tradition. These *ethical and moral standards* will derive from, at least in part, and will be consistent with the explicated convictions that the tradition holds about the reality of the divine. In this sense, then, ethics can be said to be intertwined with religious beliefs held by religious believers. These standards, however, must also be consistent with and congruent with other standards, principles, and values that adhere to all humans, independent of what religion they are, or whether they claim to be religious or not.

The distinctions that are made here are important to bear in mind in our analysis of ethics across the curriculum. Ethics in the university can be and is *developed according to both its religious and philosophical foundations,* and both vectors of analysis can provide the basis for an adequate understanding of how educators can sharpen the moral skills and tools that our students develop in their time in the classrooms of our colleges and universities.

B. Religious Belief and the Personal Worldview

One of the facts of life is that each person is unique. An aspect of our uniqueness is that each of us constructs our own sense of meaning; that is, we individually and in the context of a group or social context piece together over time a set of understandings about the way the world functions, the way we understand the dynamics and parameters of our lives, how others live in relation to our meaning structures, and a sense of which choices we will make or desire to make about the kind of life that we wish to pursue. To be human is to be meaning-making creatures. We locate our situation and our sense of self through the meaning that we both construct and discover. This construction entails both an understanding of how and who we are in the world and a sense of the ideal or what we, and the world, should and could be in an ideal way.[2]

This arrangement is described as religious in that it entails a set of insights and understandings about the nature of human existence that provide an explanatory framework for comprehending the ultimate ground and comprehensiveness of scope for the full range of human experiences.[3] Religious beliefs provide ways of answering the limit questions

(questions at the extremes of life—suffering, death, birth, mystery, and tragedy) and other basic questions that humans ask of themselves and are confronted with in the course of their experience.[4] In a religious sense, this framework is based on a set of posited and/or chosen beliefs that form the plausibility structures for the life an individual leads, and helps to explain the world in which the individual is situated. It provides a framework from which a set of questions and issues about the meaning of human life can be derived. Religion seeks to provide answers to the fundamental question about human meaning: "Who am I/who are we?"

There is a strong connection between this religious framework and the range of moral choices and decisions that individuals make. From a "coherentist" perspective, one that establishes the need for us to make choices that cohere with our broader understanding of reality, the moral life has meaning only as it relates to this wider personal worldview. The philosophical and theological perspectives of the two authors converge on this point to assert that the personal worldview is one that is inherently religious in that it incorporates "in principle" the fullest and most comprehensive range of personal considerations possible. This assertion provides the foundation upon which an understanding of the relationship between religion and morality can be developed.

This arrangement in a moral sense takes first the form of a factual base. What do we think are principles we can trust? What method do we have that will insure that we only acquire (as much as possible) true beliefs and not false ones? This is the stuff of epistemology. It is not our purpose here to argue for a particular interpretation of epistemology such as foundationalism, coherentism, internalism, or externalism;[5] rather, we will only bring up aspects of epistemology as they are relevant to the discussion at hand, which is the manner in which we add religion and other values into our worldviews. Let it suffice here to say that no matter how we try to create a theory of truth that is linked to a theory of epistemic justification, we are involved in a necessary human endeavor that we will term "The search for the common body of knowledge."

The common body of knowledge is that part of knowledge that links us to others; the operative term here is "common." It is a group of statements about the world that we all agree are true. These statements may be based on experiences of God that an individual or group has had; they may be derived from the common sacred texts that have served as the organizing focus for a community's beliefs about God; they may be based on the historical memory of a community over time; they may be speculative positions that form a community's worldview. There are a variety of sources of revelation in a religious sense that can serve as the organizing center of the common body of knowledge for all.

For example, in many cases the nuclear family is a robust community. When sacred texts serve as the organizing focus of the common body of knowledge within a family, within this community there are clear understandings about what constitutes a fact or value. A family may all agree, for example, that the Bible, Tanak, or Qur'an is the divinely revealed word of God (an agreed-upon fact). We may also agree upon the way to read these holy texts. However, this is not a certainty. For example, a family that identifies as Jehovah's Witness might hold the following:

1. There is a God—Fact
2. Divinely conferred immortality is possible for human beings after death—Fact
3. God forbids eating blood—Assertion[6]
4. Accepting a blood transfusion is no different from eating blood—Assertion
5. If one eats blood when alive, one turns to dust upon death—Assertion[7]
6. We know premises 3-5 to be true based on faith that a (selectively) literal interpretation of the Bible reveals God's will—Assertion
7. The eternal laws of God enjoin us not to eat blood (nor engage in any synonymous activities—such as receiving a blood transfusion)—1-6
8. If one lives a faithful life in accord with Jehovah's laws, eternal life is assured—Fact[8]
9. If one wishes to attain eternal life he or she should not eat blood (nor engage in any synonymous activities—such as receiving a blood transfusion)—7,8

This argument requires that Jehovah's Witnesses refuse blood transfusions even in cases in which a blood transfusion is the only medical procedure that might save an individual's life. This value judgment goes back to the shared (among the community of Jehovah's Witnesses) understanding of what constitutes a religious fact. In this case a fact constitutes a particular reading of selected passages of the Bible. But this reading is controversial.

In the case of the Jehovah's Witnesses, the reading of Genesis and Leviticus is about pollution caused by "eating" the blood of another. In the case of most Orthodox Jews, these passages are about food preparation in order to obey the commands of God.[9] In the case of many Catholic Christians, it is about historically situated commands based upon culinary hygiene.[10]

1. Religion, Interpretation, and the Common Body of Knowledge

So what do the Genesis and Leviticus passages (as read by these various religious communities) tell us about the common body of knowledge? Well, for one thing, it is clear that what counts as a fact differs in these religious contexts. These very same texts are interpreted differently by Jews, Jehovah's Witnesses, and Catholic Christians. This means that every "fact" must be interpreted so that its presence might find significance. Even those advocates of "literalism" bring to the holy texts a particular worldview that alerts them to what to expect when they confront a passage that appears to contradict what they hold to be true.

This level of interpretation enters in at every level. As was mentioned earlier in chapter Four, the attribution of "facts"—even in science—is not totally objective. The agent or the community is present at every level as an interpreter. Thus, when a research team in Utah claimed a simple demonstration for cold fusion many people reacted with skepticism. This is because it violated their accepted common body of knowledge.

However, the situation with science is somewhat different than the situation with religion. This is because of the principle of empirical intersubjectivity. In a dispute over what should count as a fact, say the boiling point of water at sea level, one could (in principle) appeal to an experiment.[11] The experiment (if properly constructed) will, in principle, settle the dispute. Thus, "in principle" disputes about empirical facts (though not value-free) are somewhat resolvable due to the principles of intersubjectivity and experiment.

Religious facts are different. First, in some traditions the only concrete empirical data come from the holy books. Some proponents of Christianity, Judaism, and Islam (for example) hold that the holy books should be read literally as the divine revelation of God. This goes so far in Judaism and Islam that adherents are exhorted to read the texts in their original languages (Hebrew and Arabic). This is because true translation is impossible. Whenever one translates a text from one language to another, interpretation is inevitable. There is a wonderful anecdote about a computerized translation program that had been created by the Soviet Union in the late 1980s. This translation program could take a passage from Russian and automatically put it into English. The program was put on show before the American ambassador to Moscow who was to choose a passage to test the new computer program. The ambassador chose Matthew 26:41 (the second half of the verse). This passage is generally translated into English as "The Spirit is willing but the Flesh is weak."[12] However, when a Russian Bible was found and the passage procured, the high-powered computer program rendered the passage as "The vodka is good, but the beef is rancid." This translation may have been justified on some literal principles, but it is clear that it grossly misses the intent of the passage. This is because there is more to translation than a mere one-to-one substitution of words. Thus, those Christians who claim to be literalists (yet read in translation) are involved in a problem. What are they aspiring to be literal to? The original text (the divine revelation of God), or the translation (the revelation of John Doe and his team of translators)?

This problem is even present for those who read their texts in the original. This is because paper has a limited shelf life. After so many years (300 to 500 years in ancient times) texts fell apart. There was a need for constant recopying. When texts are recopied, mistakes occur. This happens even in the most accurate settings. For example, in Islam there is a tradition that the Qur'an must never be copied unless there are two people present who know the Qur'an by heart. These individuals are supposed to supervise the task and prevent errors. But even these meticulous measures are not foolproof. In the manuscript tradition of the Qur'an there are (as in every manuscript tradition) variants that must be reconciled when one wishes to create an accurate modern version of the text.[13]

Both these small variations, in the case of reading a holy text in the original, and larger variations, in the case of reading a holy text in translation, require the reader to accept that the text she is reading is not necessarily the same *exact* text that fellow believers were reading a thousand years ago. This fact makes theological literalism a very difficult position to totally support. If this is true, then some sort of *textual hermeneutics* is required. This requires the creation of a theology that begins with the text (or common experience), moves to the dogma and doctrine of the theology, and then moves back to the text again. This dialectical process goes on until the central tenets of faith are interpreted and the most glaring textual contradictions are resolved (i.e., set into interpretive contexts that point to particular teleological resolutions).

The details of textual hermeneutics are beyond the scope of this book, but they point to one version of the process of creating a common body of knowledge that interprets what should be recognized as religious fact.

Obviously, many of these facts also imply corollary values (as per the Jehovah's Wittiness example cited earlier). Thus, the common body of knowledge contains both facts about the world and various values that follow from the acceptance of these facts. In the case of empirical facts, there is a more intersubjective flavor to these facts and values. The ethical principles elucidated in chapters 4 and 5 have this sort of flavor since they are based upon the goods that are progressively necessary for action.

However, when we confront religious facts and values, even literalists must accept that there is a difference between the epistemic justification of facts in a science book and those in a holy book. This difference lies in the intersubjective verification through experiment that exists in the former and not the latter. In the main, revelation in the religious realm is a private experience albeit in a communal context. Even the existence of public holy books that serve to organize traditions and communities of faith does not change the fact that they must be *interpreted* by each individual in the light of an understanding of a systematic theology (dialectically derived).[14] Thus, what counts as a religious fact or value is determined by each individual who, in turn, may discuss her views with another in a dialogue aimed at discovering the truth.

2.   Aesthetics, Interpretation, and the Common Body of Knowledge

The results of this dialogue in the robustly defined community at hand, family, congregation, or other unit, form the common body of knowledge so important to the creation of a Shared Community Worldview.

In a like manner, aesthetic values are also promulgated in this same fashion. One person or some community of people sees a problem with the existing way that aesthetic facts and values are being presented in a canon of criticism (analogous to systematic theology in the previous case). As a result of this dissatisfaction, the individual undergoes a re-evaluation of what should constitute authentic facts and values in art.

For example, take the romantic movement in Britain among the so-called Lake poets in the end of the eighteenth century. In the neo-classical movement that was in vogue at the time, restraint and slight nuance from traditional forms of verse—such as Pope's didactic heroic me-

ter (iambic pentameter with rhymed couplets)—was thought to be beautiful.[15]

> Hope springs eternal in the human breast:
> Man never is, but always To be blest.
> (*An Essay on Man Epistle I,* l. 95, 1733)

The act of critical appreciation began with a scansion of the prosody,
then proceeded to an examination of the end-rhymes, and finally considered the thoughts and how they were expressed. The thoughts and prosody were considered to be timeless adaptations of the Greek and Latin
classics (hence Pope's translations of the *Iliad* and the *Odyssey* and Dr.
Johnson's *The Vanity of Human Wishes*).

This all changes with Blake, Wordsworth, Coleridge, Shelley, Keats,
and Southey.[16] No longer is the touchstone the Latin and Greek body of
literature as extended into English forms exhibiting universal truths that
transcend any one person's exposition of them. Rather, the direction is
the individual elevated soul of the poet expressing a personal vision in
often-irregular prosody.

> My heart leaps up when I behold
> A rainbow in the sky;
> So was it when my life began;
> So is it not I am a man;
> So be it when I shall grow old,
> Or let me die!
> The Child is father of the Man;
> And I could wish my days to be
> Bound each to each by natural piety.
> (from William Wordsworth, "My Heart Leaps When I Behold,"
> 1807)

The personal worldviews of Pope and Wordsworth are different; what
counts as their aesthetic common body of knowledge is different. The
former accounts for the latter. In the former case the dogma of the neo-
classical critical school is accepted with all of its associated assumptions
of what counts as a fact and a value. In the latter case the romantic critical school is accepted or being developed with all of its associated assumptions. Under the worldview of the neoclassical school Wordsworth's poetry is awful. Though there is a rhyming pattern, the prosody

is very uneven. The thoughts are personal and not universal. Therefore, an acquisitions editor with the worldview of neoclassicism would have to tell Mr. Wordsworth, "Though your verse shows much promise, we cannot accept it in its present form. Perhaps you would like to consult a master poet like Alexander Pope and model your verse after his!"

This fictional rejection letter is meant to illustrate the role of personal worldview and the shared community worldview in the context of their dialectical interaction. Just as in religion, the first step is the individual's creation of a critical theory through which all art will make sense. This is in accordance with the Personal Worldview Imperative. The next step is the social interaction with another so that she, also, might enter into a dialogue about the same. At the end of the process will be a community of like-minded people who share many essential features of their common body of knowledge and the resulting community worldview.

C. Arranging Values into the Personal Worldview Imperative

So how do we go about arranging religious and aesthetic values according to the Personal Worldview Imperative (PWI)?[17] Well, the PWI has four principal components: 1) consistency, 2) completeness, 3) goodness, and 4) acting out one's beliefs. In this discussion we will assume that the religious quest is always about goodness and acting from this understanding. Thus, we will move our discussion toward comprehensiveness and coherence. However, in the last section we have treated coherence vis-à-vis the reading of holy texts in light of an interpretative theory. That leaves comprehensiveness as the salient area to be explored. This discussion will concentrate upon religious values with respect to comprehensiveness as a model by which other value integration might also occur.

What does it mean to be comprehensive regarding your religious values? This question involves one in a fundamental dispute on how wide the religious domain reaches. On the one hand there are those (let's call them the Platonists[18]) who say that every facet in life should be influenced by one's religious values. These proponents say that religion is the human response to God's dictates and that every single action we commit must reflect the presence of God. The rationale for this is that a person should not segregate his life so that only certain problems are religious. These people believe that the most important ontological entity is God. That which is most important should be reverenced out of respect of that eminent position.[19] Therefore, whatever is aligned to God must be followed.[20] God dictates principles that inform every choice; therefore, every choice should be informed by God.

On the other hand, there is the (what we shall call the Aristotelian) position that there is a natural division in the way we know and also in the nature of each entity.[21] On this second account of comprehensiveness, the dictates of God are limited. There are many instances in life in which God's dictates do not weigh in on the question. For example, there is no "God's method" for doing a calculus problem or a T-table in statistics. There is no significant difference between a person doing a proof in symbolic logic who is a theist under the first mode and a theist under this second mode—or an atheist for that matter. The point is that the mode and matter of one's belief in God is not relevant for these domains.

This second mode is rather tricky. It seems to reveal truths and untruths. The truth it reveals is that it *does* seem to be the case that the most proximate rationale for performing many actions does not rest in religion. Six times four equals twenty-four. This is true whether or not one believes in God (much less *how* one believes in God).

There are many instances such as this. Even if the first assumption were true, the *proximate* justification for believing in the truth of *p* (where *p* is some logical proposition) is not related directly to God.

Ethics across the Curriculum and the Shared Community Worldview Approach

The Shared Community Worldview Imperative states, "Each agent must strive to create a common body of knowledge that supports the creation of a shared community worldview (that is complete, coherent, and good) through which social institutions and their resulting policies might flourish within the constraints of the essential core commonly held values (ethics, aesthetics, and religion)." This imperative is important to universities that seek to promote authentic value exploration in the context of the Personal Worldview Imperative, i.e., encouraging their students to live reflective lives that seek values in ethics, religion, and aesthetics.

The first step in the process of creating a shared community worldview is creating a commonly accepted common body of knowledge. This was discussed in the first section of this chapter in the context of deciding what would count as a religious or aesthetic fact.

In many ways the setting of the university is an ideal community to practice the skills of developing an accepted common body of knowl-

edge. This is because at universities there is often a bit more of a speculative atmosphere than exists in the rest of society.[22]

One of the best ways to foster this sort of wide-ranging speculation is
for the university to encourage and support professional development of
professors through discipline-specific and interdisciplinary speaker series, conferences, and faculty research. However, no faculty development
program is complete without a tie back to the students. For it is the students who will act as seeds to germinate their thoughts in the society at
large. So often, conferences are planned or speaker series initiated that
do not contemplate the involvement of students at some level. This can
create a research setting in which faculty view their community as
merely their peers within their discipline. Students and others associated
with the university (such as the administration) are necessary evils that
must be tolerated in order to maintain their personal quest for truth.

But universities *are* communities. They are not hermitages. As communities they incur various community responsibilities. Among these are
duties to pursue a vision of what might be best for the community and to
work to reform the current vision. But this activity cannot occur in soli-
tude. It is a group effort. This group effort occurs in many venues: teaching in the classroom, department governance, school governance, university governance, and the general attitude that the university has toward its
official and unofficial missions. Each of these units is important. In many
colleges and universities across the United States, there is often a discon-
nect at some level. For example, some departments may view themselves
rather autonomously and evince disdain for the rest of the process. But
this cannot be, or else the larger community will either evolve into an
ineffectual blob or become a tyrannical bully. Neither of these alternatives is acceptable. The only way to correct this is to accept community
responsibility in some way for each and every robust community in the
university. This does not mean that every member of the classics department should sit on the faculty senate, but it does mean that the classics
department should make its presence felt in the larger community (e.g.,
university governance) in some fashion. And it also means that it should
not just be the same people over and over again assuming this burden.
The ideal is a rotating system whereby an individual accepts larger
community duties and then passes them onto others.

So where does religion fit into this community decision-making process? This is a difficult question—particularly at public colleges and universities in the United States where the constitutional sanction establish-

ing a state religion has been legally interpreted as meaning that there should always be a clear separation between church and state.[23]

This difficulty about how to treat religion in public colleges and universities is made even more complicated by the fact that religion is a widespread phenomenon in the world. If colleges and universities just pretended that religion did not exist, then they would be ignoring an extremely important part of the personal and community worldviews of most of humankind. If a university is about exploring all the aspects of what it means to be a human in the world and the truths that support that existence, then the university cannot ignore religion!

But what is the university to do about religion? How can a public college or university fulfill its official secular mission and yet not ignore the real role that religion plays in most people's lives?

One approach is the schizophrenic or "divided mind" approach. Under the schizophrenic approach the university pretends that everyone is an atheist. All its official acts would be perfectly attuned to a student body that was 100 percent atheist. The intent is to be value-neutral regarding religion. By making this assumption, it cannot be accused of promoting any particular religion. Confidentially, the university tells its students and faculty that what they do on their own time is *their* business so long as they aren't denying others of their rights of expression. The university will support, in modest ways, private groups of all sorts (not only religious but political, aesthetic, dietary, and so forth). Thus, the university says that publicly it is a religion-free zone, but it is tolerant enough to allow those who want to practice religion to do so on their "own time."

The argument for this approach is that the public college or university can claim that it supports no religion but it does not forbid private observances of the same. Under this scenario a religious group is treated in the same way as a tattooing club or a kayaking fraternity.

The problem with this approach is that to the religious (which constitute the great majority of all people in the world[24]) religious values are of a much higher sort than tattooing or kayaking. In fact, they are essential for an authentic life. Clearly the above approach to acknowledging religious value is woefully inadequate for most people. This is because the "official version" of atheism is *not* value-neutral but is, in fact, itself a religious position. Atheism (the doctrine that there is no God) and agnosticism (the doctrine that the agent is not sure whether or not there is a God[25]) are both theological positions.[26] Thus, by the state adopting a default atheistic position, it actually *involves itself* in the religious debate by taking a religious position. But what alternative is there?

One vision might be a community that accepts that most people *are* religious and that there is nothing wrong with this fact. These values are public facts and the community should recognize them. However, what about the plurality of different religions? They often dictate different values. How can the community create institutions and their resulting policies (also called for by the Shared Community Worldview Imperative) if it recognizes the conflicting commands of one religious community and another community?

This is a challenging objection and one that any advocate of the shared community worldview will have to confront. It points to the fact that it is possible that some groups cannot live in community with others on an equal basis. Since the dictates of their religious values are logically contradictory, there is no way to accommodate both in the same way and in the same respect.

The alternatives in such a situation would be: 1) Create a mechanism whereby the beliefs and activities of the minority religious group will be recognized and appreciated by the majority; 2) Find ways in which the beliefs and activities of the minority religious group can be factored into the group's decision in some sort of proportional fashion; 3) Invite the minority religious group to leave the community and go somewhere else; 4) Persecute the minority religious group (from social ostracism on the weak side, to death on the strong side).

If we agree to exclude from our examination peculiar religious groups that might advocate murder and child sacrifice (for example) and concentrate on the so-called big five—Christianity, Islam, Buddhism, Hinduism, and Judaism—then clearly alternatives 3 and 4 are unacceptable. Alternative 1 is a very good choice but it does not go far enough. When at all possible, we should strive toward adding alternative 2 because this moves us away from some sort of model of unfettered individualism to one in which the presence of a community is recognized. Most communities should have enough social "give" to allow any religion some significant presence in a community[27] that can be publicly recognized, and for the values of that religion to be taken into account in public decisions.

Even when the threshold or number of members of the religion is rather small, every effort should be made in the public sphere to accommodate firmly held religious values whenever possible. For example, in the United States, the pacifism of the Quakers was taken into account through the Selective Service classification of "conscientious objector" (even though there were very few Quakers in our society). Also, Jehovah's Witnesses are absolved from reciting the Pledge of Allegiance in public school (because the Jehovah's Witnesses believe that it violates the commandment to Moses, "Thou shall not make an idol.") Though such cases are somewhat rare, they illustrate the model of how a society ought to treat minority religions and their resulting worldview values.

In most cases, alternative 2 becomes problematic only when the scope of the accommodation is rather large and the population requesting the accommodation is sufficiently small. For example, let us suppose that there was a small group of Islamic Americans who were living in a university community. Let us also assume that this Islamic community believes that women should not exercise in the same building as men. Let us also assume that constructing athletic facilities is very expensive. Since (in this example) there are not very many Muslims in the university, then it would be (practically) unreasonable for the Muslim students at the university to expect that the university should build a separate women's athletic facility.[28] Since athletic facilities cost ten to fifteen million dollars these days, such a request creates too great a demand upon the university to accommodate a religious minority.

On the other hand, if another university had a third of its student body advocating a separate women's athletic facility due to religious values about the separation of men and women in sport, then the university ought (if it could) build a separate women's facility. This is because the proportionate representation in the community has reached a state of critical mass.[29]

Thus, to review what has been said, it is inauthentic for public universities in the United States (or any other society that espouses a separation of church and state) to believe that it is fulfilling its mission by pretending to be a religion-free zone. This is because such a position amounts to atheism or agnosticism that are themselves theological positions. The religion-free zone ideal thus promotes a religious position, viz., one of atheism or agnosticism. It is inescapable.

Given this inescapability of taking a religious stance, the university should adopt a different strategy. In this strategy the university (and any other community) should first insure freedom for all legitimate religious groups, and second (as much as is practically possible) strive to integrate those values into the Shared Community Worldview through recognizing the unique values presented by the religion in the common body of knowledge (recognized by the community). It is our opinion that this approach to religious values by the public university is superior to what is being presently practiced, i.e., the "religion-free zone."

The flip side to this question is what to do about private colleges and universities, especially those associated with a particular religion. Obviously, among the private colleges and universities in the United States of America, some act just as public universities do, i.e., to portray their mission as secular. For those colleges and universities, the above analysis of public institutions will apply.

However, there are many other colleges and universities that are associated with particular religions. It is to these institutions that our final remarks are directed. When an institution of higher learning decides to align itself with a particular religion, that part of the university's mission can play out in several ways. One of the most popular approaches is what we will call "symbols and jingles." In this approach the university or college will seek to shield itself from direct interaction with religious activity or its religious heritage. This is often due to the legitimate fear that overinvolvement might compromise the spirit of free and unfettered intellectual inquiry that is essential to institutions of higher learning.

As a result, the symbols-and-jingles approach will engage alternative 1, i.e., to create a mechanism whereby the beliefs and activities of the minority religious group will be recognized and appreciated by the majority. In addition, the university will create a symbolic iconography about campus that gently reminds students of the religious heritage of the university. In the case of Christian colleges or universities, this might take the form of crosses, doves, saints, halos, and glowing pictures of the sky with sentimental messages attached. These symbols are meant to create a low-key atmosphere of Christianity about the campus.

The same is true of the jingles. These are little phrases that pick up a small piece of some aspect of the religion. If we continue to follow in our Christian example, one might see little posters around campus proclaiming, "Love One Another," "Faith, Hope, and Love," "Blessed Are Those Who Hunger and Thirst for Righteousness," "To the Greater Glory of God," etc. The purpose of the jingles is the same as the purpose of the symbols: to convey compact, representative aspects of the Christian worldview as understood in that community.

The way such symbols and jingles are understood depends upon whether the viewer is of the same religion or not. If a Christian sees a cross or a slogan or the Greek letters *XP* she thinks little about it. It is a familiar sign but does not stir much emotion pro or con. If a non-Christian who is tolerant of Christianity sees these signs, she thinks about it a great deal and tries to find a place in her soul to accommodate such symbolism. If a non-Christian who is not tolerant of Christianity[30] sees these symbols and jingles, then she is reminded once more of how she is alienated from the community she lives in. It is one more vehicle of alienation.

The advantages of the symbols-and-jingles approach is that it is the least obtrusive approach. It soft peddles a message that few will actually attack as patently offensive.[31] The disadvantage of the symbols-and-jingles approach is that it doesn't really engage those who believe in the university's religious heritage (e.g., Christians in a Christian college or university). And it may act to alienate those at the school who are not tolerant of the university's religious heritage (generally because they come from a different religious heritage).

The second approach is religious indoctrination. In this approach everyone in the university or college is made to absorb large doses of the dogma, doctrine, and practice of the religion. Following in the example from Christianity, this would mean things such as (a) mandatory attendance at Christian religious services (though not the taking of Communion unless one has been confirmed), (b) mandatory classes in Christian theology, and (c) the required acceptance of a community worldview that does not bend to the non-Christian's beliefs/needs. Some schools of this ilk will also impose codes of conduct based upon the community's understanding of what it means to be a good Christian upon all students and faculty—Christian and non-Christian alike.

The advantages of this second approach center around the claim of authenticity. Proponents of the indoctrination approach claim that only by "living their faith" fully and integrating their religion into all areas of the curriculum can they actually create a religious community. These advocates would decry the symbols-and-jingles approach as being too jejune.

The disadvantages of the indoctrination approach resemble the advantages. The detractors will generally agree that the only way to really come to know a religion is to live it in a more complete manner, however; though this may be fine for those in seminary or nuns and priests living in community, it is not what most people want in a university. They are not going to college to gain the inner truths accessible only to those who demonstrate religious commitment and devotion. Instead, they are seeking to major in math, psychology, or politics for the purpose of personal growth and to be able to get a job at the end of the line.

For these detractors, the indoctrination approach is not appropriate for general liberal arts education. For those who seek enhancement of a particular religious worldview above all else, this approach will work well. But it is not for the mainstream student.

The final approach is the one we recommend. It seeks to adopt the integration of alternatives 1 and 2 as discussed earlier: 1) Create a mechanism whereby the beliefs and activities of the minority religious group will be recognized and appreciated by the majority; 2) Find ways in which the beliefs and activities of the minority religious group can be factored into the group's decision in some sort of proportional fashion. In the case of traditionally religious institutions, this means giving rein of religious expression to all groups in the college or university community that seek to find ways to worship while at school. It should not really matter to a Christian school (for example) if a Muslim group on campus wants to use university space for their Friday prayers. Some religious schools (though far too few) actually lend their chapel to Muslims for Friday prayers, to Jews for Saturday services, to Christians (in most cases the sponsoring institution) for Protestant and Catholic observances, and to Buddhists for Dharma talks.

In this way, a traditionally religious school makes a statement that it is about promoting the observance of religion. The school may officially set out that Christianity (for example) is best from the institutional point of view, but this does not imply that others are "bad"—only not "as good." However, because the school is, in fact, advocating religion, they are viewed as valuable. By supporting other religions, the institution sends a message to the student that the university promotes spiritual exploration (even if it is not the official religion of the college) as an important part of being an educated person. This is a powerful message.

Detractors of this third way would say that (from the point of view of the indoctrination approach) it does not go far enough in promoting the religious traditions of the university. They might also say that there is only one single way to salvation and that this third way obscures this fact by embracing all religions into the community.

Detractors from the symbols-and-jingles approach might claim that this third way is too much engaged in promoting religious activity. Better the soft-peddled that is less intrusive.

Yet, from the point of view of the Personal Worldview Imperative and the Shared Community Imperative, a university that has as part of its mission the heritage of a mainline religion and does *not* encourage members of its community to explore and grow through their religious values is failing its students.

Proponents of this third way will contend that it provides an alternative that has many of the advantages of the first two approaches while not endangering academic and intellectual freedom. This caveat is very important since universities throughout history have not exhibited a very good track record on academic and intellectual freedom in a religious setting.

What we propose is a direction for both public and private colleges and universities that allows that portion of the personal and the shared community worldview imperatives to be expressed in ways that nurture religious growth in a context of intellectual freedom.

Notes

1. This classification and analysis of the general typology of religion and theology is based in large measure on the work of Richard McBrien in *Catholicism* (Minneapolis: Winston Press, 1980).

2. The idea of meaning here is taken from the work of James Fowler, particularly *Stages of Faith: The Psychology of Human Development and the Quest for Meaning* (San Francisco: Harper & Row, 1981).

3. The theology of Paul Tillich is the basis for the religious claims made here. See in particular *The Courage to Be* (New Haven: Yale University Press, 1980).

4. The idea of "limit-questions" is central to the work of David Tracy's philosophical theology in *Blessed Rage for Order* (New York: Seabury Press, 1975).

5. There is an enormous amount of material written on each of these approaches. What follows is a quick introduction to each. For foundationalism see William Alston, "Two Types of Foundationalism," *Journal of Philosophy* 73 (1976): 165-85; Roderick Chisholm, *The Foundations of Knowing* (Minneapolis: University of Minnesota Press, 1982); Ernest Sosa, "The Foundations of Foundationalism," *Nous* 14 (1980): 547-64. For coherentism see Keith Lehrer, *Knowledge* (Oxford: Clarendon, 1974) and Nicholas Rescher, *The Coherence Theory of Truth* (Oxford: Clarendon Press, 1973). For internalism see Richard Feldman, "Reliability and Justification," *The Monist* 68 (1985): 159-74; George Pappas, ed., *Justification and Knowledge* (Dordrecht, Holland: D. Reidel, 1979). For externalism see Alvin Plantinga, *Warrant and Proper Function* (Oxford: Oxford University Press, 1993).

6. Genesis 9:3-4, cf. also the reading of this passage by Watch Tower Bible and Tract Society of Pennsylvania, *Family Care and Medical Management for Jehovah's Witnesses* (New York: Watch Tower Bible and Tract Society of New York, 1995).

7. The consequences of disobeying God's command in this respect are that a person will be cut off from God; see Leviticus 17:10, 13, 14; 7:26, Numbers 15:30-31, Deuteronomy 12:23-25.

8. This example comes from Julian Savulescu and Richard W. Momeyer, "Should Informed Consent Be Based on Rational Beliefs?" *Journal of Medical Ethics* 23 (1997): 282-88.

9. For a discussion of the role of divine commands in the observance of ethical/religious duties see Michael Boylan, *Basic Ethics* (Upper Saddle River, NJ: Prentice Hall, 2000), chapter 6.

10. This is the case because Catholic Christians (for the most part) do not follow the rules of practice. Further, the Catholic understanding of the Mass (Communion) is about the essential change of bread and wine into the Body and Blood of Jesus. This would mean (in one sense) that Catholics are blood eaters every time they partake of the sacred elements. Therefore, in a fundamental sense, Jehovah's Witnesses view the "facts" of biblical revelation differently than do Catholic, Anglican, and Orthodox Christians.

11. However, it must be acknowledged that the principal level of disagreement from an objector's point of view will often focus upon the experimental apparatus. In this case the measuring device is critical. There was a tortured history in the development of the mercury thermometer. This is because there is so much at stake in which medium one chooses for the fluid in the thermometer tube. Each substance has very different characteristics. The choice of substance reflects one's theory of temperature. For example, as a former athlete, Boylan can attest that in his experience in sports, when it became hot, each increment upward counted for *more* than one—as per his race in Fresno, California in 1968 at the temperature of 110 degrees Fahrenheit, when Boylan suffered fifteen large blisters in the mile run. If it had been a few degrees less, Boylan declares, he might not have suffered any! Thus, if we took the attitude that a thermometer should move between temperate extremes evenly, but then change radically when human comfort is compromised, a different fluid than mercury would have been chosen. Why should we have a measuring device that is uniform through – 100 and +120 (as mercury is)? This is due to a theoretical bias on the nature of temperature, viz., that it must be uniform. But if subjective experience is the key (à la Berkeley), then another fluid might have been chosen.

12. As per *The New Oxford Annotated Bible: New Revised Standard Version* (New York: Oxford University Press, 1994).

13. For an overview to some of these issues see Arthur Jeffrey, ed., *Materials for the History of the Text of the Qursud, Ubai, Ali, Ibn, Ibn Abbas, Anas, Abu Musa, and other early Qurtext of Uthman* (New York: ABS, 1975).

14. Keith Ward makes this sort of argument in his Gifford Lecture, *Religion and Revelation: A Theology of Revelation in the World's Religions* (Oxford: Clarendon Press, 1994).

15. An example and account of changing poetic tastes as seen through neo-Aristotelian criticism can be found in R.S. Crane, *The Languages of Criticism and the Structure of Poetry* (Toronto: University of Toronto Press, 1953), 54 ff.

16. For a classic overview of these changes see Albert S. Gerard, *English Romantic Poetry, Ethos, Structure, and Symbolism: Wordsworth, Coleridge, Shelley, and Keats* (Berkeley: University of California Press, 1968).

17. In the interests of a concise presentation, the rest of the chapter will concentrate upon religious values. However, a similar set of arguments could also be constructed concerning aesthetic values along the line of the last section.

18. The key text for this attribution is the analogy of the sun and the allegory of the cave in *Republic,* book 6, 508a ff. In these passages, Plato uses the sun as the symbol for the form of the Good. Some Christians, Muslims, and Jews have interpreted the form of the Good to be God. In the passages, various objects (meant to be the other forms) are only "seen" because of the light of the sun. We can only know ultimate reality through the divine grace of God. Just as the sun illumines the object of sight in our lives, so also does God illumine the objects of internal reflection. In an unreflective mode we do not realize that what we see is only possible because of the sun's light (n.b., before electricity). Without the sun there is no vision. In an unreflective mode we do not realize that what we understand is only possible because of God. Without God we are nothing. If this quick gloss correctly depicts one position, then God would necessarily be involved in every action we take.

19. Some would rephrase this as respect for the supreme *power* of God. However, this second formulation is more complicated because it involves the question of *why* might makes right or whether there is a difference in this formulation in general or when it might be applied to God, cf. Plato, *Republic,* book 1, 336c ff.

20. Sometimes this takes the form of divine command theory. See Boylan, *Basic Ethics,* chapter 6.

21. It is important to note that this artificial and somewhat superficially drawn distinction is at the metaphysical level only. One could concentrate upon other branches of philosophy—such as ethics—and bring Aristotle over to Plato's side. For example, character ethics (often attributed to both Plato and Aristotle) would seem to support the first alternative. Also, one might use Plato's logical theory of division (see the *Statesman*) to make him an advocate of the second alternative.

22. This is certainly not meant to suggest that universities are perfect bastions of disinterested reflection. To the contrary, it is often the case that petty turf battles are fought harder in universities than in society at large. However, despite this caveat, the university has as its mission the support of speculation and intellectual inquiry. This is just the sort of fertile soil for the growth of a rich common body of knowledge.

23. This is, of course, a tortured question. Some of this controversy is discussed by Darien A. McWhirter, *The Separation of Church and State* (Phoenix, AR: Oryx, 1994).

24. Though such statistics are very difficult to compile since it is difficult to determine what (in some cases) constitutes a religion and what is merely a cultural artifact, the *Time Almanac 2000* (New York: Information Please, 1999), 404, says that 72 percent of the world's population is either Christian, Muslim, Hindu, Buddhist, or Jewish. That is a substantial majority that increases as one counts Sikhs, Jainists, et al.

25. As a matter of practice, most agnostics work on the principle of "sufficient reason," meaning that unless there is a sufficient reason for believing in some proposition *p*, such as "God exists," then the proposition will not be believed, cf. William Kingdom Clifford, "The Ethics of Belief" in *Lectures and Other Essays,* vol. 2 (London: Macmillan, 1901): 163-205. Now, it is one thing to say "God does not exist" and another to say "I do not believe God exists, because I am not aware of a convincing argument for the same"—however, in practice both amount to the same thing.

26. They are theological because they address the existence and nature of God. Theology is first and foremost about the existence and nature of God. The examination of the mode (if any) of God's existence is a traditional category for theological discussion. Anyone who asserts that God does not exist is thus entering the theological arena (even if she did not mean to do so).

27. For purposes of education, many U.S. educators use the threshold of 5 percent for accommodating the minority group at the expense of the majority. For example, how do we know how many religious holidays are appropriate for secondary schools to recognize by closing school? If one religious group is 5 percent or greater in a school district, that is sufficient to include its most holy days in the official school calendar.

28. This would count as a case in which (because of the size of its population) the group's claim for a new athletic arena (a secondary good that ranges from medium to low-medium) is less embedded than the university's ability to use funds to provide a sound education to its students (a deeply embedded basic good).

29. What is the magic number of critical mass? This is a tortured question that is beyond the scope of this discussion. However, let it suffice that the answer probably depends upon the accommodation requested. The more drastic the accommodation, the higher the necessary proportional representation. This is not an entirely utilitarian calculation but rather a recognition that not *every* request can be met. Those with a large monetary cost must be seen in the context of the percentage representation of said group within the overall community.

30. One might legitimately ask the question why a non-Christian who is intolerant of Christianity is attending a Christian school. The answer probably lies in

the fact that such a student did not attend the school *because* it was Christian, but *in spite of* the fact that it was Christian.

31. This is not always the case. Donahue, while dean of students at Georgetown University, found great resistance to the display of crucifixes around campus. Because a crucifix is more graphic than a simple cross, there was quite a brouhaha.

Chapter 8
From Theory to Action: Ethics
across the Curriculum

In Chapter 7 we discussed the role of the common body of knowledge as a critical element in the Shared Community Worldview Imperative. The focus in that chapter was upon religion and other values—such as aesthetics. Here, we intend to highlight the direction this might take in the university as we reintroduce ethics to our discussion.

In order to facilitate our discussion, let us borrow from business ethics the concept of a stakeholder. Under this sort of analysis, a corporation (or university in our case) is depicted as a collage of relationships that includes virtually any agent or group that owns, works for, or is affected by the company or its policies. The "stake" is the interest, share, or claim that an agent or group has against some company. Those who possess these stakes whether they be legal, economic, political, moral, etc., are called stakeholders.[1] This way to view the corporation is called stakeholder theory.

R. Edward Freeman depicts stakeholders as "any individual or group who can affect or is affected by the actions, decisions, policies, practices, or goals of the organization."[2] Under this model we can distinguish between primary stakeholders of the company (owners, customers, employees, and suppliers) and secondary stakeholders (all other interested groups such as the general public, government, and competitors). Primary stakeholders weigh more heavily in the decision-making process than secondary stakeholders, but even primary stakeholders possess stakeholders of their own, so that the societal web becomes very complex.

Proponents of stakeholder theory point to the way that it *situates* a company. That is, it forces the company to view itself as being contained in a series of environments that often intersect. In this way, a company must (as much as possible) accommodate its actions with the needs and interests of all of its stakeholders. If morality is about ameliorating one's own interests given the broader group's interests (a crucial tenet of utilitarianism), then stakeholder theory creates a means of integrating ethics into daily business decisions.[3]

For our purposes we will call primary stakeholders in the university: the students, the faculty, the administration, any and all groups directly doing business with the university (suppliers, companies working in co-operative grants, grant-making agencies—including the federal government), individual donors, the president, and the governing board. Secondary stakeholders will be other universities, alumni, prospective students, and others in the general public who are substantially affected by the university's actions.

Primary Stakeholders

When a university or college decides to make ethics a pervasive aspect of its mission, then each of these stakeholders must be brought into the picture. Let us examine a few of these in order to sketch out how such a vision might be put into effect.

First, let's begin with the faculty. Traditionally, ethical analysis has been the purview of the philosophy and theology or religious studies departments. They are the only scholars on campus (for the most part) who have studied ethics on the post-graduate level. They are the most aware of the nuances of meaning that are often so important to ethical discussions. However, if we leave it at that, then we will never really get ethics across the curriculum. This is a problem.

There are probably a number of solutions to this problem. But let us suggest just a few. First, one can create a long-range plan for faculty development. This might include something like a faculty development seminar that is open to faculty across the university. Both of the authors worked on such a seminar for six years at Marymount University. Participation in the seminar was competitive, based upon application. Participants were given a stipend for their work. The seminar lasted for one week (six hours a day). There was a significant prereading component to introduce the participants to the basic principles in philosophical ethics. The seminar was strategically positioned to occur just after spring graduation.

The purpose of the seminar was to 1) introduce faculty from disciplines other than philosophy and theology to basic concepts in ethical theory; 2) explore with faculty from the professions the ethical issues and professional duties that are meant to be a part of the practices of each profession; 3) explore with faculty from humanities and sciences how values permeate what they might believe to be positivist disciplines; and 4) work on ways to introduce ethics into each class in a natural way (each participant finished the seminar with a teaching module that might be used directly in a class).

It was hoped that participants in the seminar might use the skills and knowledge acquired in the seminar to introduce ethical issues into their normal classroom discussions. Secondly, the participants might use their experiences to affect their discipline's curriculum design (i.e., to include ethical components). Finally, participants might interact more effectively in their professional associations through their ability to include aspects of ethics in their teaching. Thus, the terminal objectives of the seminar were to affect the teachers in their present teaching, departmental curriculum design, and their larger professional community as represented through various national and regional associations.

After six years we have decided to change the direction of the faculty development, trying to incorporate the following goals:

- The faculty ethics seminar should be continued in some new form.
- The faculty ethics seminar should create a level of participation for former seminar participants.
- The faculty ethics seminar might include summer faculty development projects. These grants would only be available to those faculty who have already taken the faculty ethics seminar. These might be accompanied by grants that would match summer school teaching stipends (obviously with the proviso that the recipient not teach summer school).
- After research ethics grants have been awarded, there will be a meeting of all principals in order to coordinate efforts and to utilize alumni of the seminar in the execution of the current seminar.
- The traditional form of the seminar—i.e., a prereading segment, a presentation of the major theories segment, a discussion of professional practice, and a participant project that is presented to the group—should be continued with the inclusion of seminar alumni in the process.

Thus, the second phase of the project intends to move faculty to another level of involvement in their use of ethics in the classroom and in their professions.

This approach is obviously just one attempt to bring the faculty into the process of ethics across the curriculum. There are probably many others that will work as effectively or more effectively depending upon the college or university. However, this case study is one attempt to integrate the faculty of the institution into the vision of ethics across the curriculum.

The next primary stakeholder to examine is the student. How does the ethics across the curriculum proposal affect him? Many of the same challenges that were outlined in chapter 2 (from the faculty's point of view) also affect the student. In one way, introducing ethics into all the courses in the university can be seen as a distraction (if the material is not integrated into the basic concept of the course) or as an enrichment (if the material is presented in such a way as to enlarge the context of the course). Students have a deep need to feel that what they are learning is relevant to something. What the something is can be various. It can range from (a) being relevant to the requirements of the major and relevant to getting a job from that major, to (b) being relevant to becoming an expert practitioner of whatever profession (and its practices), to (c) being a *eudaimon* (balanced soul) person in the world. Most often, students (these days) are more excited over (a) and (b) than they are over (c). But that does not mean we should ignore (c). It is our job as educators to promote a developmental experience that is in the best interests of the students from a comprehensive vantage point. Thus, we should be promoting (a), (b), and (c).

From chapter 6 we know that professionalism depends upon creating an ethos or worldview that is good. This is in accord with the Personal Worldview Imperative. Each person becomes a better practitioner at what she does by being cognizant of the social, political, and ethical consequences of her action. This is, in once sense, a consciousness-raising activity. But on the deeper level it is an empowerment program that seeks to better the quality of how we all behave toward each other.

To do this the student must believe in the cause. The only way to get this sort of commitment is for the institution to make it clear from the outset that the university or college really believes in promoting individual ethical reflection and action (Personal Worldview Imperative) and dialogue and community action (Shared Community Worldview). How does this happen?

As in the case of the faculty as a primary stakeholder, there is no magic formula. But three strategies that have been effective are (a) essay competitions on ethical case studies, (b) speakers that are accessible to a general undergraduate audience, and (c) conferences of undergraduates presenting papers and entering into discussions on topics of ethical import.

For an undergraduate ethical case study essay competition to be effective there needs to be publicity to the entire undergraduate population. Generally, some sort of cash prize acts to enhance student interest. Also, the criteria for an effective essay must be widely distributed. Finally, there should be workshops offered by ethics scholars so that interested students might be able to hone their skills in writing case study evaluations.

What an annual undergraduate ethical case study essay competition can do is to entice students into evaluating the ethical dimensions of real situations "all by themselves."[4] In the best of all possible worlds, there would be a number of cases that the students could evaluate—each of which represented a variety of disciplines/professions. In this way the student could focus upon her discipline/professional knowledge as part of the case study evaluation.

The second area of student development is a speaker series that is accessible to general undergraduates. So often, speaker series are really directed at faculty development. The speakers are those who present their most recent journal articles for general discussion and debate. But far too often these talks are not accessible to the general undergraduate student. For this reason, these talks are most often populated by the faculty and by the star students in the discipline—but very few general undergraduate students.

The creation of an undergraduate speaker series along with ample opportunity to interact with the speaker in a positive, nonthreatening manner will allow students to think about various ways that others are approaching ethical dimensions (and other values such as religion and aesthetics) involved in the practice of any discipline/profession. Students tend to give more credence to outside speakers than to their own faculty. (This is the "a prophet is without honor in his own land" syndrome.) Thus, a good speaker series with adequate devices for feedback and reflection can be an effective tool in bringing ethics across the curriculum.

The final tool for bringing students into the picture is to promote conferences of undergraduates presenting papers and entering into discussions on topics of ethical import. The number of undergraduate conferences seems to be expanding. In many cases these conferences are aimed at majors in philosophy or theology (or some other discipline-specific audience). However, this need not be the case. In the Washington, D.C. area for example, there has been an annual undergraduate conference on peace and conflict resolution. This is indeed a topic that resonates across various disciplines. Papers and panels are set up topically so that a number of perspectives might be given on a single question. This is certainly a very positive step. It requires the creation of a common body of knowledge (often achieved very quickly in the course of the session) and the resulting discussion of how one discipline's perspectives might be understood and evaluated by another. Certainly the sort of shared community worldview dialogue advocated in this book requires this sort of interaction in order to proceed in a constructive fashion.

As in the case of faculty as a primary stakeholder, these suggestions are not meant to be definitive, but rather as points of departure for future initiatives.

The last primary stakeholder that we will examine is the administration (including the president and the board). Any attempt at instigating ethics across the curriculum must include the administration. This is because it sounds rather empty to advocate one thing and then go on with "business as usual" with the operations of the university. How can the administration sign on in a significant way to the commitment to ethics across the curriculum?

A caring approach to all internal customers, faculty and students, is essential for an institution that preaches ethics across the curriculum. There is nothing more hollow than saying one thing and doing another. For example, in the United States during the 1980s and 1990s it became very popular for many businesses to adopt codes of ethics. At the very best, these codes aspired to create a direction that would lead the organization in a responsible direction. At the very worst, these codes were shallow statements that were offered without any corresponding change in behavior on the part of the company. Instead of being a good thing, such meaningless platitudes serve to make employees angry and disenchanted with the company, and cynical about ethics.

The same sort of disenchantment can occur in universities that are not careful to match their *words* with corresponding ongoing *deeds*. Such a relationship is dictated by the Personal and Shared Community Worldview Imperatives. In each case, action is stressed along with proper attitude.

Therefore, if a university wishes to espouse a policy of ethics across the curriculum, it must be prepared to back it up—not only in initiatives for faculty and students (outlined above), but also through a self-study of how the administration itself is committed to the same mission.

One way for the university administration to effect such a change in their "terms of engagement" is by creating a series of university-wide forums whereby faculty and students can air grievances on important ethical issues within a context of constructive correction. It is one thing to bemoan the way things are being handled. It is another to become a part of the solution. One way to do this is by creating teams in these university-wide discussions that work together to evaluate what actions and procedures exist in the university that go against the mission of honesty and openness. After these actions and procedures have been identified, then the team should work together to brainstorm possible solutions to these problems.

After the small-group sessions, there could be a general convocation in which the observed problems and the recommendations are presented in a larger group setting. Finally, an executive committee should take these disparate reports and consolidate them into an action plan that is put into effect in a very public fashion.

This sort of exercise is good for the administration to engage in because it creates a procedure whereby the ideas of internal customers are recognized. It also creates community by linking students, faculty, and administration together in a process designed to improve commonly shared problems. This sort of exercise should be repeated with some regularity (say yearly) until there is a real sense of community and common purpose about the university's policies and procedures (usually implemented by the administration).[5]

The third thing the administration can do to implement ethics across the curriculum is to make visible and public its support of the initiatives mentioned in the faculty and student sections above. There are many subtle ways that an administration can honor those engaged in the effort to bring about not only a curriculum change, but also a fundamental alteration in the way business is done at the university. It has some of the earmarks of a revival movement that seeks to make the university not just another pedestrian public institution, but a positive source for good: a transforming agent to affect society at large. Universities don't exist for themselves only, but also for the sake of the society that supports them. If the university can encourage and nurture the idealistic youth that will go forth into society and "change the world" for the better, then it is doing what it should be doing.

Of course all of these lofty goals cost money. In this case money is needed to support faculty and student initiatives. This money might be visibly raised in a restricted endowment fund. Now, some may say that every dollar that goes to such a restricted endowment fund comes out of the pocket of some other university program. Such an analysis would be true if the number of donors and the amount of their donations were a fixed universe. In such a possible world every dollar set into a new fund would be a dollar diverted from another fund.

Luckily this is not the case. There are many donors who are interested in associating themselves with ethics programs—especially those that are as wide-ranging as we are proposing. In this case, the money pledged to the restricted endowment is new money that otherwise would not have come to the university. However, there is the legitimate point that the *time* spent raising this money is time that *could have been spent* raising money for other university programs. If it is thought that other university programs are more primary to the university's mission, then detractors might contend that the time spent raising money for a restricted endowment in ethics is time spent away from the university's principal duties. This argument would contend that such an ethics program might actually weaken the university because by siphoning away time from development personnel, the net effect is to decrease total spending in other areas more primary to the university's mission.

There are two responses to such a charge: (a) it is untrue that ethical awareness and involvement is less primary to the university's mission, and (b) it is very possible that if alumni and the general community are included in the overall implementation of the program, then total contributions to the university may rise both inside and outside the restricted endowment. Ethics education must be viewed as central to a college's mission.

First, we would argue that the development of the whole student is what every university is primarily about. By "whole" here we mean something akin to the robust definition of the authentic person set out in the Personal Worldview Imperative. It is not enough to create technical competence in the college and university. We must also create citizens with the responsible judgment to use their expertise. This harkens back to our discussion of professionalism in chapter 6. Part of being a professional is not only mastering and submitting to the practices of the profession, but also being responsible stewards of this power. The most essential way to foster this sort of development is through the ethics education that we propose. This ethics component must be integrated into every discipline so that each graduate of the university leaves with the tools to become a more responsible citizen. This terminal objective of producing not only technically competent but also responsible citizens should be at the heart of every university's mission statement.

Secondly, if the university actually stands for something like the promotion of the examination of values both through its primary stakeholders and through its secondary stakeholders, then there will be a certain audience who will pay attention and support such efforts with donations. We speculate that these will not be restricted to the ethics program alone, but will spill over and include an endorsement of the entire university. Thus, the end result may very well be more contributions for all the university's programs.

What the university or college does by earmarking some of their fundraising personnel to the cause of a restricted endowment for ethics across the curriculum is to show by an outward and visible sign an inward direction toward a more complete way of educating our students. Actions speak louder than words, the old adage goes, and it is no more true than in the case of a university taking the plunge and devoting internal resources toward the creation of a restricted endowment for the purpose of supporting this program.

Secondary Stakeholders

The second category of stakeholders applies to other universities, alumni, prospective students, and those in the general public who are substantially affected by the university's actions. All of these constituents are also affected by a university that has committed to ethics across the curriculum. Let us briefly examine how these respective stakeholders might view a college's decision to commit to ethics across the curriculum.

Other Universities. All universities exist in a context. This context includes the society at large and other universities. Among the other universities, those who exist in the same competitive universe are the most influential. For example, if X is a somewhat selective state university that is classified as a comprehensive university, then the behavior of a very selective private university that is a Ph.D.-granting institution is somewhat irrelevant. Each institution is concerned with different problems. Each draws upon a different pool of students (in the main).[6] But if we look at institutions that draw upon a similar demographic population, then the actions of one will influence the actions of another.

This dynamic can work for the good or for the bad. In the case of the bad it might mean a lowering of standards or of the quality of education. If one university in a competitive universe changed the way it admitted students (for example), or the way it graded its students (eliminating the D grade or easing grading standards), or other such things, this could ripple through the comparable schools in that universe and affect them, as well.

But there is also an upside. On the upside, one might affect the competitive universe in such a way that the standards are raised. In this case one university might offer a value-added service (such as early admission) that proves so popular that it catches on with other schools. In this way ethics across the curriculum might in the short term be reflected only in isolated schools (with no seeming impact upon these secondary stakeholders), but in the long term, it might change the way we think of educating our students.

Alumni. Alumni are an interesting group of people. At one time they were primary stakeholders, but now they are secondary stakeholders.[7] However, though this may be the case, they are secondary stakeholders who have a real interest in the continued development and reputation of the school. If Mr. X got a degree from university Alpha and subsequently university Alpha rose from prestige level 3 to 5 (on a scale of 1 to 5), then automatically X's status has been enhanced. (No one asks what Alpha was like when X went there.)

Now consider Ms. Y, who attended university Beta. Beta has gone from 5 to 3. Ms. Y has been injured by the loss in status for university Beta. (No one asks what Beta was like when Y went there.)

In these examples it is clear that alumni are affected more than most secondary stakeholders in the fate of their alma mater. When we consider the impact of a university adopting ethics across the curriculum, the alumni will be in favor of it if they perceive that it enhances the university's reputation and will be against it if the opposite is true.

The only way that ethics across the curriculum (in our opinion) could be considered in a negative vein is when critics claim that the extra time spent on ethics is at the expense of the meat-and-potatoes issues of traditional disciplines.

Our response to such an attack is that the university is not just about producing technocrats. The mission of the university is to produce whole, caring people who are decent and competent in their fields. 'Excellence' in this case is about more than learning how to be a statistician according to traditional textbooks. It entails more. It requires statisticians of high personal character and integrity.

Prospective Students. This group of secondary stakeholders frequently comes to the university in a daze. The United States does not properly prepare students for what it might be like to attend college A or college B. Many students are attracted to a school by its sports teams—even if they are not going to play on those teams. Since the American society does not revere its colleges and universities as such, but rather accepts them as means to an end (generally a job), it is important for universities that have accepted the commitment of ethics across the curriculum to make this new end (value development) a selling point for these individuals. This is also the fair thing to do. This is because if you want to infuse your university with ethics, then (at least in the beginning phases) the prospective student will acquire a different education than her peers at comparable institutions. If the university truly believes that this approach is valuable, then it must go out on a limb and advertise itself to prospective students for what it is. Let those who are attracted come, and those who are turned off look to another college.

The General Public. This is the final group in the secondary stakeholders that we are highlighting. The so-called town-and-gown friction has occurred since the advent of the modern university in the twelfth century. Much of the resentment that often occurs between schools and their non-academic neighbors may be eliminated by the inclusion strategy. For hundreds of years, various colleges and universities that have experienced tension with the general community have tried strategies of inclusion. This means inviting the general public to be a part of the university's various activities—such as were outlined above in the faculty and student development sections.

When the general public is welcomed into the university[8] there is the potential of a positive and harmonious relationship. If the university has committed to a policy of ethics across the curriculum, and if the general community is involved, then there is the possibility of extending the transformation of the single unit (the university) to its environment. What a powerful thing it would be for a dialogue to begin between the general public and the members of the university community on the subject of ethics and values. The entire enterprise might go a ways toward renewing our public worldview.

In conclusion, we have tried to set out an argument that has as its kernel that the modern university should transform itself from a mere set of segregated disciplines (each pursuing its own version of truth) to a more integrated institution that employs the values espoused in the Personal and Shared Community Worldview Imperatives to shape a new direction. This direction is inclusive, holistic, and embraces ethics, religion, aesthetics, and other values.

We live in a world of crisis and increasing confrontation based merely upon techno-superiority and power. If we continue to follow this path, we will be doomed. Let us set the universities at the vanguard of a renewal in the other direction based upon ethics across the curriculum. It just might change the world.

Notes

1. For a further discussion of the definition of stakeholders see Archie Carroll, *Business and Society: Ethics and Stakeholder Management* (Mason, Ohio: South-Western Publishing Company, 1989), and Joseph Weiss, *The Management of Change: Administrative Logics and Actions* (New York: Praeger, 1986).

2. R. Edward Freeman, *Strategic Management: A Stakeholder Approach* (Boston: Pitman, 1984), 25.

3. One need not put forth a utilitarian model here in order to employ stakeholder analysis. For example, the authors lean toward virtue ethics and deontology as their preferred ethical theories. In the case of virtue ethics, one could imagine character traits and practices that emerge from the worldview of the community. These might be accommodated via a community dialogue. In the case of deontology, stakeholder analysis might bring to light moral duties in the way that discussion on the common body of knowledge sharpens the shared understanding of the basic goods of action (and one's resulting duties).

4. The "Ethics Bowl" competition for undergraduates directed by the Association for Professional and Practical Ethics is a good model for universities to consider.

5. Of course, this example will have many different implementation structures depending upon the size of the institution. A small college can create a close general community, whereas a larger university must depend upon smaller groups that affiliate in some recognizable fashion with a larger whole.

6. Obviously, these two institutions might draw upon the same group of undergraduate students, and therefore their interaction at this level might be different than their interaction at the graduate level.

7. Of course there are those alumni who maintain a very close affiliation with the university, taking on leadership roles in various capacities. Let us classify these individuals as part of the administration; thus, they remain primary stakeholders.

8. Sometimes this "welcoming" requires a bit of prodding as well.

Appendix 1
Getting Started: Some Frequently Asked Questions

Q: Must we set up an ethics institute in order to create a program of ethics across the curriculum?
A: No. In fact, we recommend that the best way to start is with a small committee of interested individuals within the university who will get together and give their support to creating a faculty ethics seminar. This seminar (ideally) should contain someone within the university and someone outside the university.

Q: What happens to the committee after the seminar is planned and broad support is achieved?
A: The committee can be ongoing, meeting once a month, and will (eventually) be the core of an advisory board to an ethics institute, should that turn out to be a vehicle that the university will support.

Q: What about follow-up to the ethics seminar?
A: This depends upon the support that the university or outside funding agencies are willing to give. Team teaching with members of the philosophy or theology department(s) is one alternative (with the content person as the lead and the philosopher/theologian as the support person). If this sort of funding is not available, then some sort of feedback session in the fall and spring semesters would be useful to keep the vision clear, give mutual support, and talk about common problems.

Q: What about other programs?
A: Other programs such as conferences, community events, and student research initiatives may develop as individual circumstances (and resources) permit. The most important thing to do is to form a faculty committee, plan a seminar, and *get started*!

Appendix 2
A Structure for a Faculty
Ethics Seminar

The following is the structure of the seminar used by the authors.

Participants
We thought a mix of 6 to 8 faculty from various schools was best so that a broader sense of ethics in the context of the university's mission might be obtained. For the first year, many of the participants should come from the faculty steering committee (see appendix 1). After attending the first iteration of the seminar, these initial attendees can be advocates to their peers to attend the seminar.

Length of Seminar
The seminar that we did lasted one week: Monday through Thursday, 9:00-3:00; Friday, 9:00-12:30. We have talked to people at other universities and some of them ran two-week seminars for 12 to 15 faculty, in the morning only. This is a matter of taste, but having a longer, intense seminar often makes a stronger impression upon the participants.

Stipend
This will vary from institution, but for a one-week commitment we found $1,000 adequate.

Schedule of the Week
Prereading
    Basic Ethics, Michael Boylan
Monday
    9:00-12:00 Overview, discussion of expectations, key terms, strategic thinking with the group; assignments for the week given
    12:00-1:00 Lunch
    1:00-3:00 Ethical Intuitionism and Virtue Ethics; Theory and Cases
Tuesday
    9:00-12:00 Utilitarianism and Deontology; Theory and Cases
    12:00-1:00 Lunch

1:00-3:00 Religion and Ethics, Professional Ethics, Intertheory
Cases, Narrative and the Carriers of Worldview and Ethos
Wednesday
9:00-12:00 Participant presentations on the normative character of
their disciplines/professions (with interactive discussion)
12:00-1:00 Lunch
1:00-3:00 Participant presentations on the normative character of
their disciplines/professions (with interactive discussion)
Thursday
9:00-12:00 Participant presentations on their teaching modules (with
interactive discussion)
12:00-1:00 Lunch
1:00-3:00 Participant presentations on their teaching modules (with
interactive discussion)
Friday
9:00-11:00 Participant presentations on their teaching modules (with
interactive discussion)
11:00-12:30 Alumni presentations (in the first year we engaged in a
follow-up to the strategic-thinking discussion on Monday), goals
for the future discussed

Appendix 3
Internet Resources

It is always a tricky thing to put into print (a more permanent medium) that which is very mutable (the Internet). However, at the writing of this book the following sites should help those interested in this topic interact with others around the country who are following models that have worked for their schools.

http://www.rit.edu/~692awww/seac/ [accessed November 1, 2002]. The Society for Ethics Across the Curriculum. This is a dynamic, new organization that promises to create a clearinghouse for those interested in starting something at their schools.

http://www.dartmouth.edu/ [accessed November 1, 2002]. General site for Dartmouth College. Navigate to their center for ethics.

http://www.fairfield.edu/ [accessed November 1, 2002]. General site for Fairfield University. Navigate to their center for ethics. Lisa Newton has been a pioneer in this area.

http://www.iit.edu/departments/csep/eac/eac_index.html [accessed November 1, 2002]. One of many sites associated with Illinois Institute of Technology.

http://www.rit.edu/ [accessed November 1, 2002]. Rochester Institute of Technology. A rich site. Wade Robison is the director for the Society for Ethics Across the Curriculum.

http://www.slu.edu/centers/ethics/activities.html [accessed November 1, 2002]. The University of Saint Louis is very active in ethics across the curriculum.

http://www.towson.edu/ [accessed November 1, 2002]. Towson State University is a solid site to visit.

http://www.unlv.edu/ [accessed November 1, 2002]. University of Nevada at Las Vegas is an active member of the Society for Ethics Across the Curriculum.

http://ethics.acusd.edu/eac/ [accessed November 1, 2002]. The University of San Diego and what they've done. Lawrence Hinman has been very active in ethics and the use of technology to get the message across.

http://www.uvsc.edu/ethics/eac.html [accessed November 1, 2002]. Elaine Engelhardt has created a very comprehensive program at Utah Valley State College. It is well worth the visit.

http://www.wiu.edu/ [accessed November 1, 2002]. This is the general site for Western Illinois University. Navigate to the ethics programs.

http://www.wmich.edu/ [accessed November 1, 2002]. This is the general site for Western Michigan University. Navigate to the ethics programs.

http://www.ysu.edu/ [accessed November 1, 2002]. This is the general site for Youngstown State University. Navigate to the ethics programs.

Index

Universities and colleges
Comfort-level problem, 31-33
Common body of knowledge, 27,
    57, 68n, 116-22, 123, 127, 133n,
    137, 142
Communication, 47-48
Communitarianism, 106
Community, 123-31, 139
Completeness, 66, 122
Comprehensiveness, 57, 58, 115,
    122. *See also* Worldview,
    Personal Worldview Imperative
    & shared community worldview
    imperative
Conn, Walter, 55n
Consistency, 45, 58, 64. *See also*
    Worldview, Personal Worldview
    Imperative & shared community
    worldview imperative
Constellation theory, 49-51
Continuity in ethics, 46-47
Conversation, 47-48
Convictions, 48
Cook, Mark L., 110n
Cook, Martin, 110n
Correction, 47
Crane, R.S., 133n
Cronkite, Walter, 32-33
Cultural expressions, 22, 26, 44,
    48, 113
Curran, Charles, 50, 56n

Dalai Lama, 18n
Damokos, G.K., 35n
Damokos, S., 35n
David, the king, 61
Deal, Terrence, 55n
Deontology. *See* Ethics, deontology
Descriptive ethics. *See* Ethics,
    descriptive
Deuteronomy, 132n
Disciplines and ethics. *See* Ethics,
    disciplines
Divided mind approach, 125
Dodds, E.R., 69n

Dolly (the sheep), 29
Donahue, James A., 54n, 110n,
    135n
Donaldson, Thomas, 111n
Duty, 72-73, 75, 78-79, 84, 87, 89n
Dworkin, Ronald, 111n

Education, 2, 108; constellation
    theory, 49-51; curriculum, 4, 21-
    36, 143; ethics, 3, 7, 8, 17, 108,
    137-48; general, 9, 15; liberal
    arts, 2, 8, 16; professional, 15,
    24, 91-109; purpose of, 3, 143;
    role of the university, 4, 107,
    143; whole person, 4, 15
Eigo, Francis A., 19n
Egoism. *See* Prudential
Embedded-values approach, 71-89;
    table of, 80-81
Engelhardt, Tristram, 54n
English literature, 22-23, 64
Erikson, Erik, 54n
Ethics: across the curriculum, 4, 15,
    21-36, 105, 138, 142; applied vs.
    theoretical, 8; character, 43-49,
    104-105; classroom, 13-14, 139;
    codes, 96; constellation theory,
    49-51; deontology, 63;
    descriptive, 11; disciplines: 14;
    biology, 23, 28-30; business, 15,
    64-65, 92, 108; chemistry, 27-
    28, 36n, 64-65; classics, 124;
    engineering, 91; English, 22-23,
    64-65; interior design, 24; law,
    14, 89, 107-108; math, 129;
    medicine, 109; natural science,
    14; nursing, 91, 92; politics, 129;
    psychology, 129; physics, 28;
    duty, 72-73, 75, 78-79, 84, 87,
    89n; education (*see* Education,
    ethics); fact-value problem, 21-
    27, 63; intuitionism, 63;
    narrative, 37-56; normative, 10,
    60, 63; vs. metaethics, 10;
    philosophical, 10-11, 63, 114;

About the Authors

Michael Boylan (Ph.D. University of Chicago) is professor of philosophy at Marymount University. He is the author of *Basic Ethics* (2000), an essay on normative and applied ethics, and *Genetic Engineering: Science and Ethics on the New Frontier* (2002, with Kevin Brown), along with thirteen other books in philosophy and literature and over sixty articles.

James A. Donahue is President and Professor of Ethics at the Graduate Theological Union, Berkeley. His work in *Ethics across the Curriculum* is based on his experience of sixteen years as professor of theology and ethics and dean at Georgetown University, Washington, D.C. He has published *Religion, Ethics, and the Common Good* (with Theresa Moser, 1996), along with other chapters and articles on professional ethics, foundational ethical theory, and religion and public life.

Made in the USA
Middletown, DE
04 March 2020